Porn Addict's Wife

ADVANCE PRAISE

"Finally, there is a book written by a spouse about porn addiction. Sandy Brown offers an important voice to the conversation about this "new" addiction. *The Porn Addict's Wife* is a well-researched, personal account of the heartbreak of this ever-growing, marriage- and soul-destroying affliction. As she describes her own denial, discovery, and recovery process that helped both her husband and herself, she allows the reader to identify with the incredibly difficult feelings and steps that must be faced in order to truly heal from the insidious persistence of porn addiction. Sandy's book is practical, useful, and heartfelt. Fortunately her story is one of hope and healing, which will give the reader strength to overcome the most difficult challenges on the road to wellness. As a psychotherapist, I am relieved and grateful to have such a helpful, easy-to-read, guide for my patients."

Deborah Meints-Pierson, LMFT

"A great read with a strong message of hope and understanding for any woman who has been betrayed and hurt by a husband struggling with sexual addiction."

Thomas Shelder, LMFT, CSAT, CMAT, SRT

"Addiction and shame go hand and hand. Where there is shame, there is the urge to hide. Which breeds isolation, self-loathing, more shame, and more addiction. Sandy is my hero. In *Porn Addict's Wife* she courageously and unapologetically shines a light on one addiction that has been hidden for far too long—the addiction to pornography, an addiction that nobody has wanted to talk about. Because of Sandy's bravery, her story will heal many women who have been suffering in silence. The only way to break the cycle of addiction is to shine a light—a loving and non-judgmental (but also non-BS) light—on addiction. Sandy is a lighthouse. Her light blazes a trail, opening up awareness, dialogue, and healing for those who are affected by porn addiction."

Amy Pearson, LiveBrazen.com

"*Porn Addict's Wife is s*traightforward, direct, compassionate, hopeful, informative, inspirational, and courageous! As a marriage and family therapist, I see many women who struggle with the betrayal of their husband's porn addiction and who feel alone and isolated. Candidly telling her story, Sandy provides hope for her readers that they too can rise above the shame and survive their emotional pain when they bravely walk a path to recovery. Major thumbs up!"

Jana Rockne, LMFT, LPC

"This book is highly informative and explains in depth the issue of porn addiction and its mental, social, and emotional implications for the addict and all associated with the addict. *Porn Addict's Wife* not only sheds light on the issue of porn addiction but also highlights the road to healthy recovery. Sandy delivers a powerful message clearly and very lovingly. Through self-work and self-growth a healthy happy life is indeed possible. A fantastic read!"

Dr. Suparna Bakaya

"Sandy Brown is a beautiful light for so many women and couples with this book. She is bringing voice to an issue that so many couples face and few talk about, and she is bringing it to our awareness without shame or blame. I believe *Porn Addict's Wife* is a gift to women and their partners, offering them a positive pathway to reconnect."

Lea Ann Mallett, Action and Results Coach

Porn Addict's Wife

Surviving Betrayal and Taking Back Your Life

SANDY BROWN

NEW YORK
NASHVILLE • MELBOURNE • VANCOUVER

Porn Addict's Wife

Surviving Betrayal and Taking Back Your Life

© 2017 Sandy Brown

All rights reserved. No portion of this book may be reproduced, stored in a retrieval system, or transmitted in any form or by any means—electronic, mechanical, photocopy, recording, scanning, or other,—except for brief quotations in critical reviews or articles, without the prior written permission of the publisher.

Published in New York, New York, by Morgan James Publishing in partnership with Difference Press. Morgan James is a trademark of Morgan James, LLC. www.MorganJamesPublishing.com

The Morgan James Speakers Group can bring authors to your live event. For more information or to book an event visit The Morgan James Speakers Group at www.TheMorganJamesSpeakersGroup.com.

ISBN 9781683503835 paperback
ISBN 9781683503842 eBook
Library of Congress Control Number:
2016920071

Cover Design by:
Chris Treccani
www.3dogdesign.net

Interior Design by:
Chris Treccani
www.3dogdesign.net

In an effort to support local communities, raise awareness and funds, Morgan James Publishing donates a percentage of all book sales for the life of each book to Habitat for Humanity Peninsula and Greater Williamsburg.

Get involved today! Visit
www.MorganJamesBuilds.com

DEDICATION

To my husband, Ted: Thank you for your unconditional support in going public with our story, and in joining me to overcome the shame of porn addiction so that our story can make a difference in the lives of others.

TABLE OF CONTENTS

INTRODUCTION:

Trapped in Pain

Shocked.

That's an understatement when it comes to discovering your husband is a porn addict. In fact, many women have no clue that porn addiction is even a thing. You may have felt there was something different about your husband, but couldn't quite put your finger on it. Maybe you were suspicious he was having an affair, so you started searching his devices for evidence. Or you just happened to check your computer's browser history and discovered endless links to internet porn. Either way, you're probably angry, hurt, reeling, and wondering if your marriage is over.

I get it. I've been there.

The discovery of your husband's porn addiction can make you feel uniquely alone. It is important for you to know that yours is not an isolated case. Your husband is not the only man playing with fire because of porn addiction. Many women are feeling just as you are right now. Like you, they feel betrayed. Their hearts are breaking, and they feel their lives have been shattered into a million pieces. Their marriage feels like a lie, and they are mad as hell. Worst of all, they feel trapped in pain with no way out.

You have come to the right place. Here, you will find a way out of your pain. You will see that you can survive, and that you can take back your life.

Porn addiction is a huge and growing problem in societies around the world—and no marriage is immune from its destruction. It doesn't matter if you have been married thirty years or six months. Porn addiction impacts couples who have great marriages, and those who are barely getting along. It turns up in surprising places—ministers and pastors are no different than your husband, and many of them, too, are at risk for ruining their marriages because of their own porn addictions.

Even storybook marriages are affected.

My client, who gave me permission to share her story with you, had one of those storybook marriages. To protect her privacy, I'll call her Sue. From the outside looking in, her life looked perfect. Sue is supermodel gorgeous. Her husband, who I'll call Tom, is better-looking than George Clooney. Their kids are beautiful, athletic, and intelligent.

Women wanted to look like Sue, and they wished they had a husband like Tom. Tom was a prominent business leader and a pillar of the community. They had the perfect home, drove luxury cars, took dream vacations, and went to church every Sunday. Sue was a devoted wife. You know the saying, "Behind every great man is an even greater woman?" Sue was that woman. Any man would have been lucky to have her for a wife.

Sue thought she had a great marriage—until things started to change. They were just small changes at first, but taken all together, they added up to Sue's sense that something was not right. Tom grew distant from both Sue and the kids. For the most part, he lost interest in having sex with her. On the rare occasions when they did have sex, he experienced erectile dysfunction. Sue could see that Tom was very stressed because his business was in trouble, so she attributed all their relationship issues to his anxiety.

Then, Tom's behavior changed so much that Sue barely recognized him. Tom became even more distant, he and Sue grew further apart, and suddenly, his business was on the brink of bankruptcy. This is when Tom's world fell apart and his porn addiction was exposed. Sue was shocked and devastated. She didn't even know there was such a thing as porn addiction. Tom ended up ruining his reputation, his business, and his family because of porn. Sue's story demonstrates that this happens even to beautiful people with beautiful lives.

I have worked with wives who were married to their childhood sweethearts and, after thirty or more years together, were stunned to find their husband had become a porn addict. A few of these husbands had been hiding their addiction so long that it escalated to full-blown sex addiction. For these men, their addiction was no longer satisfied by internet porn alone, so they took the leap to using prostitutes or other sex partners, who could easily be found online.

Some of my clients knew their husbands were using porn and didn't think much about it. They thought, "I'm so tired from chasing after the kids all day... at least he isn't bothering me." Or they thought, "Porn is a stress reliever for him, it's harmless." After letting their husband's porn use slide for a time, they suddenly woke up to realize their husband was completely disconnected from their relationship. Some wives are left thinking, "What happened to the man I married?"

Many women have been in your shoes. While the circumstances may be different, the sense of betrayal and devastation is the same. One thing most wives have in common is the way they react to discovering their husband's porn addiction. Your husband might be trying to make you think you are over-reacting, but you are perfectly normal in feeling the way you feel.

The reason I wrote this book is because my husband betrayed me. My husband had his own secret addiction that nearly ended our marriage. Nothing could have prepared me for this kind of pain, even though I had ended my first marriage because of a different kind of addiction, and I was raised in an alcoholic home. But the pain from those experiences did not compare to the emotional pain I felt as a result of my husband's porn addiction.

Wives are affected by their husband's porn addiction on a very personal level. Porn addiction seems dirty, and many wives are disgusted by it. For some reason, his addiction makes *us* feel ashamed. It is not uncommon for a wife to think that her husband turned to porn because there's something wrong with her, or because she's not pretty enough, skinny enough, sexy enough. The most common question I get asked is, "Why was I not enough for him?"

If you are thinking thoughts like these, STOP IT!

You did not cause it. You did not create it. You cannot cure it. You need to know, in your heart, that your husband's porn addiction has *nothing* to do with you. It doesn't matter what you look like, how you have treated him, how often you had sex with him, or whether you could bend yourself into a pretzel during sex. You are not the reason your husband uses porn. Nothing about you has anything to do with his problem. This may be very difficult to accept right now, but it is the truth.

Porn is a drug. Your husband is a drug addict. As with any drug, porn rewires the brain in response to the flood of natural "feel-good" chemicals that are released. The brain doesn't differentiate between porn, cocaine, crack, heroin, or alcohol. With habitual use of any drug, the brain will learn to crave that drug. That neurological craving is very intense, and is what brings the addict back to the drug. You will learn more about this in chapter two. For now, I only want to touch on the neurological changes going on in your husband's brain to help you understand that there is more going on with him than meets the eye.

Once upon a time, your husband had a healthy brain with two perfectly functioning systems that worked together to ensure his survival needs were met without jeopardizing his safety. These systems are referred to as the *go* system and the *stop* system. They are designed, respectively, to sense a need, and then weigh the consequences for fulfilling that need.

In the porn addict's brain, the systems are broken. The *go* system is in hyper-drive, and has been rerouted–even rewired–to bypass the *stop* system, making it very difficult for the user to say no. Your husband's brain has been tricked to think it needs porn, and that craving convinces your husband that he *has* to have it and can't live without it. This is your husband's brain talking, not his heart, and his brain has been hijacked. Without treatment, your husband cannot control the craving because his brain controls *him*.

This is not to make excuses for your husband's behavior. But I think it is necessary for you to understand the science of addiction because it will help you to separate yourself from his problem. With this information, it is my hope that you will begin to shift your thoughts from "what's wrong with me" to understanding what is driving his behavior.

You have probably confronted your husband by now. Maybe you've dropped his phone in the toilet, ran over his laptop with your car, or maybe even smashed his desktop with a baseball bat. Your husband may have reacted with the typical porn addict's response: "What's the big deal?" He doesn't know what to do, so he denies he has a problem. His secret addiction has been exposed, and he does not know what the hell he is going to say. He may have even gone silent.

His reaction does not necessarily mean that he doesn't care. I have no doubt he can see your pain. If he has the slightest bit of conscience left, he is in his own kind of hell. But don't expect him to have a sudden revelation. Porn addicts don't usually "get it" until they start a recovery program where they will be with men who have been through it. They will tell him how it really is, and they won't put up with any lame excuses.

All of this is great information, but I have a feeling your burning question is, "What do I do now?"

Quite simply, you take charge. This may take every bit of energy you have and may seem like more than you can handle, but I encourage you to step up and take control of the situation. It is time for you to figure out what you need in order to feel whole again. It is up to you to tell your husband what you need him to do in order to correct the pain he has caused. He does not get to call all the shots. This is your life, and you get to decide how you will proceed.

You may want to pack your bags and run as far away as you can get. I understand. If there is any threat of physical violence or any threat to your safety, I want you to call for help or get out, right now. *Your emotional health and safety are your number one priority.* If this situation has exacerbated any pre-existing health condition, seek help from your doctor or mental health professional.

If your circumstances are relatively stable and safe, I encourage you to take time before you make any life-changing decisions. Wait until you get your feet firmly on the ground. You don't have to have all the answers right now. Give yourself time, and stick with this process to find your next steps.

Now is the time to start your journey from discovery to recovery. Your quickest way out of hell is to pick yourself up and start moving forward. Each chapter you read will be a step in the direction of your healing.

Part of your recovery is to understand your husband's addiction. This knowledge will give you the authority to fearlessly take control of this situation and to tell your husband what he needs to do if he wants to be in your life. Then you will learn how to start taking care of yourself. Everything in this book is for your benefit and for your healing.

I am not a sex addiction therapist. I am not a counselor. I am a Certified Life Coach who has been where you are right now. I have walked through the fire and made it to the other side. I don't just talk about it; I lived it. Recovery isn't easy. By way of my own hard work and dedication to recovery, I have carved a path for you. I have guided other women along this path to discovering that they were survivors, and that they had the power to take their life back. Walk with me now, and I will guide you in finding your way through recovery.

CHAPTER 1: Discovering Your Husband's Porn Addiction

Not in my wildest dreams did I ever think my husband, Ted, would be a porn addict. I had absolutely no idea he ever used internet porn. I was clueless about the fact that internet porn was so accessible, and I had no idea that it was possible to become addicted to it. My idea of porn use was watching a DVD with your partner in order to spice things up a bit, and we had absolutely no need for that. Why the hell would my husband be using porn?

From the time we first started dating, my husband and I had a great relationship. We knew each other as kids and were reintroduced as adults by a mutual friend. We both had recently gone through toxic divorces, and had divorced for similar reasons. I had three sons; he had two. We had a lot in common and, most importantly for me, he seemed to be the opposite of my ex-husband.

We were both interested in personal development, and I'm going to be honest: there is something incredibly attractive about a guy who is willing to improve himself. There were many synchronicities between our lives. Being a woo woo kind of girl, I believed the Universe was bringing me a match made in heaven.

For the first time, I felt emotionally supported by a man. Ted wasn't the jealous type, and he didn't try to control me as my ex-husband had. He accepted me unconditionally and loved me with all my quirks. Ted had integrity, and for me that was really important.

We took our time and dated a few years before we decided to take the big step of blending our families. In 2007, we married with our five sons in attendance. Blending a family is not for the faint-hearted. There are all kinds of problems to work through, but even considering all our challenges, we had a strong marriage. Most importantly, I knew I could depend on him to be there for me no matter what. I had never truly felt this with any other man, and for me, this made all the difference in the world. I never had to worry about betrayal with Ted. He was true blue.

Our marriage wasn't perfect, by any means. We had our share of fights. There were times when we could go for days without talking to each other. But more often than not, Ted would extend the olive branch and we would work through whatever issue caused the fight in the first place.

We spent most of our free time together, and were rarely apart. (I wonder–where did he find time to use porn?) One of Ted's most endearing traits was that no matter the circumstances, if I was in need, he would drop whatever he was doing to help me. When I called, he answered. When I texted him, he replied. He was always there for me.

Then, slowly, he started to change.

They say hindsight is 20/20. Looking back, I can clearly see the red flags. But at the time, I had no idea he even looked at porn. The changes were subtle: He was becoming more distant, was less involved with the family, and was more argumentative. The biggest change was that he was less interested in sex with me. He didn't seem like the same man I married.

As time went by, these issues became more pronounced, and there was no way to overlook them. I would wonder if I was crazy, or imagining things. Something just wasn't right, and a voice deep inside was telling me so. But you know how it is when we ignore that inner voice. We tend to justify our fears away: "This is normal. Everything will be ok. Don't make something out of nothing."

Eventually, the change in Ted became impossible to ignore. I was out of town visiting one of our best friends, Jennifer. Ted would have usually come with me, but he chose to stay home because he said he had to work. It was a beautiful summer day, and Jennifer and I were enjoying our first beach day of the season. Then, in one misstep, we were in a crisis situation that lead to Jennifer going to the hospital via an ambulance.

I'll spare you the details. Suffice it to say that this turned out to be a traumatic and stressful day for both Jennifer and me. We were in the emergency room for hours, and the entire time, I was trying to reach my husband. I needed him by my side, and I knew that as soon as I called him, he would drop everything to come.

But it didn't happen that way. I must have called him about 30 times during those six hours in the ER. He did not answer one call. This had never happened in the nine years we had been together. This was the man who *always* answered my calls. I was getting a little worried about him and was wondering what the hell was going on.

The crisis was over before he finally returned my call. When I asked him what was going on, he had some lame excuse that didn't really make sense. I asked him—even begged and pleaded with him—make the two-hour drive to join me, but he wouldn't. This was my husband who had never let me down. WTF! Who was this guy?

This is when I became seriously suspicious. For the first time in our nine years together, I did not trust my husband. I was sure he was having an affair. Nothing else could explain his behavior.

When I got back home, I even asked him point blank if he was having an affair. He denied it and looked at me like I was crazy. His response: "I would never do that to you. I'm not that kind of guy."

But, his assertions didn't satisfy me. My guard was up, and my eyes were open. Over the next couple of months, I set out to find the evidence that would prove he was having an affair. I searched his emails, his text messages, and phone logs. I compared our phone bills to his phone's logs to see if he was deleting anything. There was no evidence to be found, and yet I still had the strong feeling that something was wrong.

Ironically, the only thing I didn't think to check was the browsing histories on his devices.

Then, quite unexpectedly, everything I needed was at my fingertips. In fact, my husband unwittingly handed me the evidence himself.

One day, he brought me his cell phone and asked for help in pulling up an image that he needed to send in an email. He wasn't very tech savvy, so I started digging into places where I thought the image might have been stored.

BAMM!!! There it was! The proof I had been looking for. The proof that there was someone else in his life. There was his collection of porn videos. Porn was his mistress. I was shocked and completely blown away. In that very moment my life changed forever.

A lot has happened in our lives since that day. Ted has been working on his recovery program, and I on mine. We are both healing, and our relationship is stronger than ever. Even so, three years later, I still sometimes have questions that I need Ted to answer. One question in particular pertains to the crisis that day with our friend, Jennifer. I have asked Ted this question many times over the past three years, but I never felt he gave me an honest answer.

Recently, I asked him again: "Why didn't you come to me when I needed you?"

He replied, "If I was to go to you, that would mean I couldn't be with my porn. That is the power of porn."

Signs Your Husband Is a Porn Addict

I will caution here that occasional porn use does not constitute addiction. This is a list of the most common signs that identify porn abuse and addiction. Any of these signs, by themselves, don't necessarily mean your husband is addicted to porn. There could be other underlying issues at play. However, if you find yourself saying yes to most of these signs, your husband may well be a porn addict.

1. *Your husband has lost interest in having sex with you.*

This may sound counter-intuitive. You would think your husband couldn't get enough sex, and that is why he is addicted to porn. But his brain is craving the high from using porn, not from having sex. Or you might think you didn't satisfy him somehow, and that is why he has turned to porn. This isn't true. My husband and I had a fantastic sex life! We both felt that the sex we shared together was the best sex we ever had, and we were having plenty of it. Neither bland sex nor lack of sex is the cause for a man's porn addiction. Most guys masturbate on a regular basis. Even the most innocent may happen across internet porn and think, "Why not?" But with repeated use, it doesn't take long before addiction sets in for those who are susceptible. Once his brain becomes addicted to the high from porn use, it doesn't matter how much he loves you or how good you are in bed. His brain craves the variety and the high that porn provides.

2. *His sexual tastes have changed.*

Is he asking you to preform sexual acts that are out of character for your normal sex play? Is he more demanding and or more rough in bed? During sex, does he talk to you in a fashion that is crude or demeaning? This is not to say that "talking dirty" during sex or trying new positions is a bad thing. But if you find his words out of character or demoralizing, these could be red flags. Eventually, porn addicts try to act out in their real world the behaviors they see in their fantasy world.

3. *His performance isn't what it used to be, and his lovemaking has become selfish.*

Porn teaches men to be selfish. It is all about their high. Your pleasure no longer matters, and you are merely a means to deliver the high. Has intimacy changed between you and your husband? Do you feel like you are being "screwed" rather than being made love to? Have you ever found yourself saying or thinking afterward, "I'm glad that was great for you, but what about me?" Husbands who were once considerate love makers may now only care about their own climax.

Another side effect of porn addiction is erectile dysfunction (ED). You may have noticed this and attributed it to his being too drunk, too stressed, or too tired. There are many causes of ED, but it's also true that porn addicts often can't get an erection with normal sex. Some need to watch porn as a prelude to having sex. Others may not need the porn to become aroused, but find they can't stay erect during sex. Vanilla sex doesn't provide enough stimulation for a brain that is accustomed to the variety and intensity of internet porn.

4. *He is emotionally distant, withdrawn, and displaying mood swings.*

Even-tempered men become argumentative and sometimes ill tempered. Ill- tempered men become even more so. Where a man was once very engaged with family and friends, he becomes disengaged. Porn addiction can lead to a great deal of shame in the user. This can make him distant, reactive, and critical of you. He may pick fights or react in ways that are out of proportion to the circumstance. After having been in an argument with you, it also gives him justification and the feeling of "deserving" to go use again. It is a crazy cycle: shame to distress to acting out to relief and back to shame to distress to acting out to relief and back to shame again. You get the picture. For the addict, the cycle is like being on a hamster wheel with no way to jump off, especially when his mind has a way of convincing him, "this will be the last time."

5. *He is secretive, defensive, and his explanations just don't add up.*

They want to keep their secret world a secret at any cost. When caught in peculiar situations, their behavior and explanations for it just don't add up. And if you question their fidelity or loyalty, they react indignantly, even saying or implying that you are crazy or being insulting.

6. *Your husband is more anti-social.*

Like any addict, his focus is on getting high. Above spending time with you, the kids, or his friends, a porn addict's priority in life is finding time when he can be alone to use. If it is out of character for your husband to bow out of social engagements and he seems to be doing it more and more often, this could be a red flag.

7. *He is critical of your appearance.*

This one is painful. But even this really isn't about you. His brain is conditioned to respond to the PhotoShopped, artificial bodies of girls who are barely eighteen. Even those bodies are nothing more than objects for his pleasure. Porn has trained his brain to look for unnaturally big boobs and plump asses.

8. *He spends unusual amounts of time online.*

Some husbands are very secretive and sneaky about their internet porn use. Is your husband spending a lot of time in the bathroom with his phone? Whether your husband works from home or goes to the office, it might surprise you that the highest traffic to internet porn sites occurs between the hours of 9:00 a.m. to 5:00 p.m. Does your husband stay up for hours using the internet after you have gone to bed? Does your husband spend an inordinate amount of time in his home office after hours? If you have any questions about your husband's internet porn use, check the browser history on his devices.

9. *His devices' browser histories are empty.*

Bingo!!! While some husbands aren't so tech savvy as to clear their history, others may be covering their tracks this way. Either way, this is a great way to verify your hunch. Check his computer, tablet, or phone. With the exception of those men who are normally security-conscious, who clears their browser history on a regular basis? Clearing it once in a while would be reasonable. But if your husband is suddenly clearing his browser history every day, this might be a red flag. Another sign to look for is password-protected access on his devices. Granted, some men may have jobs where this is required. But this might be another clue that your husband has something to hide.

10. *His financial patterns have changed.*

Are there unexplained charges on your husband's credit cards? Are his bank statements not adding up? How about new credit cards? There is plenty of free porn online, but as porn addiction escalates, the addict needs more intense internet porn, the kind he'll have to pay for. For some porn addicts, their habit has escalated to a level where they need live interaction with prostitutes or random sex partners in order for their brains to get the hit. If his addiction gets to this level, his porn addiction is a BIG problem.

Now that you have read this list, you may be connecting the dots with your husband's behavior. If you are still unsure, keep your eyes open and pay attention to the signs. Secrets don't stay hidden for long. Often, the deeper men fall into addiction, the more careless they become. Their secret finds a way out.

Is Porn Cheating?

The only person who can truly answer this question is you. What does it feel like to you? If you are feeling betrayed and that your husband's porn use is cheating, your feelings are all that matter. And you are not alone in feeling this way. Most women feel in their hearts that porn use is cheating. The addict will deny, deny, deny—insisting he is *not* cheating on you when he uses porn.

Just as any drug addict will justify and defend his problem, the porn addict is blind to his addiction. You'll get the standard denials: that "everyone" does it; that it's just an image on a screen; that he didn't touch anyone, he's just looking; even that he is doing you a service by using porn when you're too tired for sex.

For the porn addict who has progressed to acting out with live partners, they have other excuses, such as "I just watched while the prostitute did _______ and I masturbated without touching her." Or this: "It was just sex, I don't feel anything for her." Here's the thing: even porn recovery programs view porn as infidelity.

From my personal experience, my heart, my mind, and every cell in my body know that porn *is* cheating. Discovering my husband was a porn addict was every bit as devastating as it would have been to find out he had been with another woman. As bad as it was, with discovery I did get to experience one tiny flash of relief when I realized, *I'm not crazy.* But that was followed quickly by the thought, *I wish I were crazy.*

If you're like me, your emotions are all over the map. Me, I wanted to strangle the bastard. My inner savage came out, and there was no controlling her. I was filled with so much pain, anguish, hate, and rage—and there was no holding it back. The hate and contempt I felt for him was like nothing I'd ever known.

In that moment, in my eyes, he was a disgusting human being. How could he do this to me? How could he do this to us? How could he do this to our family? He was cheating on me. He had taken something sacred from me and from our relationship by turning to someone/something else. I felt violated and betrayed. I felt he had trashed our relationship.

In that first rush of rage and betrayal, I felt like we were done and our marriage was over. In my mind I felt I had nothing left to lose—I wanted to get back at him and make him feel the pain of betrayal, too. I acted on this by getting all dolled up and going out on the town with a friend. I was looking for attention. I wanted to know that I was attractive to someone. I wanted to know I was desirable. But deep inside, I knew I didn't want to be with another man and, if I were, it would only make me feel worse. Instead I drank my sorrows away, and spent the night at my girlfriend's house.

At least he would have to worry. That was something.

After the initial rage settled, a new onslaught of self-inflicted pain erupted. "Why wasn't I enough?" "What is wrong with me?" The negative script in my head was more than happy to provide proof of why I wasn't enough and cited a laundry list of my flaws.

This hit me especially hard. I had been struggling with my weight for a few years. I was struggling with my own issues around self-esteem and self-worth because of it. I thought my weight gain was the reason he'd turned to porn. Those women he was jerking off to looked nothing like me. In fact, those skinny blondes with big boobs looked more like his ex-wife than me, which added a whole new dimension of pain to my story. All the co-dependency issues that I thought were behind me reared their ugly head once again.

From an early age, I had learned to rely on my looks, and that my value was dependent upon my beauty. This was a core belief that I had suppressed to my subconscious, but it was always there in the driver's seat. *If you aren't skinny and attractive, you have no value.* My husband's porn addiction brought all this to the surface, and it hurt like holy hell. His addiction was my fault because I'm not good enough.

We all have these false beliefs, don't we? Our laundry list of flaws is readily accessible from our subconscious mind, waiting for an opportunity to rise to the surface. I don't care if you look like Heidi Klum. If you have an underlying struggle with self-esteem, self-image or self-worth, your husband's porn use will give you all the more reason to beat yourself up. I know I am not alone in this. For me, this whole situation brought up a firestorm of shame and self-deprecation.

The last thing I wanted was for anyone to know about my husband's porn addiction, so I suffered in silence. I was stressed out to the max and having panic attacks, which were totally new to me. I couldn't work, I couldn't sleep, and I couldn't eat. Routine tasks felt impossible to do. I couldn't concentrate and couldn't function normally. I obsessed over thoughts of him using porn. I felt regret for having married him. How could I have fallen in love with a man who was so vile as to become a porn addict?

Discovering that your husband is a porn addict brings up a barrage of emotions and feelings, with the most common one being betrayal. Wives feel like their lives have been scattered in every direction, and they have no idea how to put them back together.

Here is a checklist of feelings. Circle the emotions that apply to you.

- ✓ Shock
- ✓ Rage
- ✓ Anger
- ✓ Denial
- ✓ Devastation
- ✓ Betrayal
- ✓ Outrage
- ✓ Disgust
- ✓ Depressed
- ✓ Anxious
- ✓ Confused
- ✓ Hopeless
- ✓ Helpless
- ✓ Powerless
- ✓ Shame
- ✓ Humiliation
- ✓ Embarrassment
- ✓ Scattered
- ✓ Overwhelmed
- ✓ Insecure
- ✓ Unattractive
- ✓ Inadequate
- ✓ Not Enough
- ✓ Less Than
- ✓ Unlovable
- ✓ Ugly
- ✓ Vengeful

If you relate to feeling any or all those emotions, you are not alone. It is very normal to feel any or all of these emotions, and you may be feeling them quite intensely. You have been traumatized from this betrayal. This experience may also trigger past traumas and may possibly even leave some feeling suicidal.

CAUTION: If you are feeling suicidal or having any thoughts of harming yourself, put this book down RIGHT NOW and CALL the Suicide Prevention Lifeline: 1-800-273-8255.

What If I Know My Husband Is Using Porn But I Don't Know What to Do About It?

If his porn use makes you feel devalued or violated in any way, his porn use is a problem. You are not crazy. You have to trust your gut. If you were able to answer yes to more than three of the ten signs your husband is a porn addict, his porn use is a problem. Stick with me and continue reading. You will learn what you can do.

It is not unusual for women to suffer in silence when they learn of their husband's porn addiction, but you do not have to stay silent. You did not cause it. You did not create it. And you cannot cure it. But what you can do is take care of yourself.

CHAPTER 2:

You Did Not Cause His Porn Addiction

I hope by now you're clear that your husband's porn addiction has nothing to do with you, no matter what he may say. Your husband is actually the only person responsible for his addiction. If you're telling yourself that it wouldn't have happened if you hadn't been so busy with the kids, or if he found you more attractive, or if you were better in bed–STOP IT! This is just a painful story you are telling yourself. Stay with me and this will become clearer as you learn more about the science of porn addiction.

When I discovered my husband's porn addiction, I wanted to learn as much about it as I could. One of the first things I wanted to know was why men use porn, but after thinking about it, I took a step back and wondered why men masturbate to begin with. Porn use seems to go with masturbation like whipped cream goes with a banana split.

Okay, so: masturbation feels good. It is a normal part of one's sexual exploration. From a very early age, kids experience arousal, though usually unintentionally. I have seen toddler boys grinding their genitals against the floor while in diapers. Little girls might experience the sensation of arousal sliding down a pole as they played on the playground. Arousal is a part of our makeup. I think it is a given that when boys hit puberty, the majority of them experiment with masturbation—that is, if they haven't been told, "You will go blind if you masturbate."

Now let's look at our husbands. They are grown adults and have regular access to sex with their wives. Why do they need to masturbate? One of the most common reasons that men cite for their need to masturbate is that their sex drive is much higher than their wife's. Maybe. But some men don't even know how to express their intimacy needs to their wife, so they masturbate instead. Equating sex with intimacy, other men feel rejected when they are turned down in the bedroom so they think it is safer to take care of themselves. They have their own emotional baggage around that. That being said, if a man's sex drive is truly higher than his wife's, it would be reasonable to see that masturbation would be an easier route to take if he wanted to avoid rejection. And sometimes, it's just faster to take care of himself.

The second most common reason men cite for their need to masturbate is stress relief. Orgasm is a common stress reliever for both men and women. For men, it is faster and easier to get stress relief through masturbation than if they have to romance their wife, and connecting to their wives isn't as efficient as hitting the bathroom stall on a lunch break. Stress in the workplace may be the reason 70% of traffic to internet porn sites occurs during the workday. It may be that the masturbation break has replaced the old-fashioned smoke break.

Even as a woman, I can relate to the stress relief factor. Have you ever come across a really uptight woman and thought to yourself, "She needs to get laid"? I've even thought it about myself. Men have all levels of stress in their lives, so I can understand masturbation being used as a home remedy to alleviate it. Men also use masturbation to deal with anxiety, sadness, loneliness, or relationship problems. Frankly, I think a guy can find just about any reason to masturbate. It has been reported that on average, men masturbate 2-5 times per week. As long as it isn't taking anything away from their marital relationship, it usually isn't an issue. But if a man is jerking off so often that it affects his ability to satisfy his wife's needs? That's a problem.

On to the burning question: why do men use porn? Men are especially visual beings and their brains are hard-wired for easy arousal. It doesn't take much for a man to get arroused. It would be a mistake to think a husband turns to porn because of what he isn't getting at home. It has nothing to do with that. Porn is about arousal. It is a fun and easy way to masturbate. Seems harmless.

I asked my husband's sexual addiction specialist, Tom Shelder, MA LMFT CSAT SRT, to share his thoughts on porn addiction. Tom is a licensed marriage and family therapist and a sexual addiction specialist. He is specifically trained as a Certified Sexual Addiction Therapist as well as a Sexual Recovery Therapist, with 20+ years of counseling experience. He told me that sex addiction therapists across the country are reporting they are increasingly treating more porn addicts than sex addicts. Tom says:

> "Porn addiction is very much like any addiction. It begins as a fun and exciting experience; but for individuals who struggle with intrapersonal issues, emotional and psychological, this fun and exciting experience can quickly turn to something dark and all consuming. The fun turns into something the addict

> is compelled to do, more and more frequently, to mask and attempt to escape the pain of the realities of life. It is no longer fun or pleasurable, but an addiction that needs to be fed."

From what Tom says, it is easy to see how using internet porn to masturbate can be a slippery slope. It doesn't take much to be aroused by porn. It can start quite innocently, but then can grow into something way bigger than the user ever bargained for. The very nature of internet porn makes it easy to get sucked into.

Soft porn is everywhere in our society. Billboards, buses, magazines, clothing ads, movies, TV shows, you name it. Victoria's Secret spends a lot of money advertising their Prime Time porn show—oops, I mean runway show. And ladies, we have to admit it: romance novels can arouse us. Raise your hand if you have read *Fifty Shades of Grey?* We might not all be masturbating as we read it, but it is arousing just the same.

Men are hard-wired to be aroused by variety and novelty. Internet porn provides an endless stream of variety, novelty, and erotic women who are always at the ready to please in the most fantastical ways. The arousal is half the fun for men. Why wouldn't porn be appealing? With very little work on his part, porn provides the arousal, and masturbation provides the orgasm. All he has to do is click a button, place his hand on the joystick, and he is off to the races, often reaching the finish line in under 60 seconds.

It isn't unusual for couples to use porn to spice up a bland sex life. I have no argument with that. It seems quite harmless. Personally, I don't have a problem with people casually using porn any more than I do with people using drugs from time to time. There are those people who can use cocaine just a few times and not get addicted. But there are others who are susceptible to substance abuse, and, before they know it, their casual use has become a full-blown addiction. Then their lives are turned upside down and inside out before they can say, cut me another line.

Some people can use porn occasionally and not become addicted. Like any drug, people begin to abuse a substance because they are using it to cope with uncomfortable feelings, emotional issues, or to avoid dealing with problems in their lives. Some drugs are incredibly powerful in taking hold of the user without the user even realizing it. Addiction sneaks up on them.

It is very similar with internet porn use. One difference between cocaine and internet porn is the way it is accessed. There is a lot of risk in acquiring cocaine. Shady and dangerous dealings have to occur in order to get the goods for consumption. Not so with internet porn. It is in your car, your bathroom, your bedroom, and pretty much everywhere you are. All you need is a device and an internet connection. You can find it and use it without anyone else knowing. Internet porn is just a click away. Most of the time, you don't even have to search for it because it will find you.

The Internet porn industry is big business. Statistics have shown that in the U.S. alone, it brings in $3 billion worth of business each year. 40 million Americans are regular viewers. Every second of every day, there are 28,000 users viewing porn. The state of Utah is the second most religious state in America, and it has the nation's highest online porn subscription rate.

Recently, a friend shared a story about a very strict Christian denomination that was holding an international conference here in the States. Many of the church's highest leaders from around the world were in attendance. The hotel venue was booked full with these religious attendees. During this event, the hotel recorded its highest porn sales, ever. Shocking, right?

Patrick A. Means, author of *Men's Secret Wars*, revealed a statistic that I find surprising: 63% of pastors confirmed they struggle with sexual addiction. The Barna Group conducted a survey that found 67% of men between the ages of 31 and 49 view porn monthly, with 50% of men between the ages of 50 and 68 viewing porn monthly. 21 million men think they may be addicted to pornography. To be fair to men, 17% of women say they struggle with porn addiction as well. With numbers like these, it's easy to see that something big is going on here. Your husband is not some freakish anomaly.

While he isn't alone, it doesn't mean he doesn't have a major problem with pornography, either. Compulsion or addiction–it doesn't matter the term, it is a big issue. It is reported that porn use increases marital infidelity by a rate of 300%. Back in 2002, the American Academy of Matrimonial Lawyers reported that 56% of divorce cases involved one partner having "an obsessive interest in pornographic websites," and 68% of divorces involved one party meeting a new lover over the internet. This is a big deal.

Statistics are great at showing us our husbands have been caught up in something bigger than meets the eye. This doesn't change the fact that you are feeling like you are caught in a tailspin. The one thing that helped me to slow the spin was to learn about the science of porn addiction. I have found some great websites with in-depth research about the brain on porn and how porn addiction effects relationships. You will find them listed on my resource page. I highly recommend you check them out.

Your husband has become a porn addict because of what is going on in his head–his big head, not his little head. Have you ever thought of your brain as your biggest sexual organ? Well, it is. I had never thought of my brain as being a sex organ at all until I started researching porn addiction.

From the point of arousal, the brain experiences a release of feel-good dopamine. All the way through intercourse and up until climax, there is an explosion of chemicals in the brain. During sexual activity, the brain is flooded with an intoxicating cocktail of dopamine, testosterone, norepinephrine, oxytocin, vasopressin, endogenous opiates, and serotonin–all perfectly blended together to create an incredible "hit" of ecstasy. Our genitals are merely the vehicles that deliver this incredible hit to the brain.

The brain loves the hit. It says, "I must make a note of how I got here so I can feel that again." As healthy adults, we learned that the path to this hit was what I call "over the hills and through the woods." While each individual has their own unique path, we have similar ways of getting there. This path may involve a variety of stimulating activities including romantic thoughts, visual cues, romantic atmosphere, intimate conversation, physical touch, and so on.

Every step on the path provides so much pleasure that we forget absolutely everything else in our world until we reach our final destination, ecstasy. Ecstasy = the "hit." You get the picture? After years of use, this path is heavily worn into our brain and becomes our primary pathway to pleasure.

There is other activity going on in the brain that is worth mentioning because it plays a role in porn addiction. I previously wrote about your husband's brain having a *go* system and a *stop* system. We all do. The *go* system evolved to help us pursue things that we needed for survival—and sex is a primal need in order for the human race to survive. The *stop* system evolved to help us weigh the consequences of pursuing whatever needs the *go* system is urged to pursue. You might say the *stop* system makes the decisions based on a logical process. When the brain is functioning normally, the *go* system and the *stop* system communicate with each other.

In the healthy brain, the *go* system has a desire to fulfill its need for sex. *Go* system says to *stop* system, "Hey, I need to have sex. Can I?" The *stop* system evaluates the circumstances to determine the possible consequences, and says either yes or no. No emotion involved—the *stop* system bases its decision on past experiences and other logical information.

But with repeated use of internet porn, all this healthy brain activity starts to get rewired, starting with the pathway to pleasure. Remember the beautiful path to ecstasy, "over the hills and through the woods"?" Porn says, "Hey, I have a short cut!" Porn basically hijacks the user's brain and takes him on a direct route to Ecstasyville!

This shortcut is a straight shot, with no hills or curves, no forests to maneuver en route to ecstasy. Taking this path occasionally wouldn't be a big deal because the path wouldn't get well-worn. However, the nature of porn being available, affordable, and anonymous makes this path a very desirable course to take often. This path is accessible no matter where the user is, meaning he can reach ecstasy anytime and anywhere.

In the beginning, the very nature of internet porn use excites the user. From the excitement of doing something that is taboo to the act of clicking and scrolling to find the perfect video, there is a release of chemicals to the brain. It is all a part of arousal. It is really hard to resist the shortcut when the brain remembers the payoff. It seems completely harmless. The user thinks, "I'm not hurting anyone else. Why not?"

Can you see how alluring internet porn is? When the user wants to get results fast with minimal effort, internet porn is the answer. This is the slippery slope. Before he knows it, your husband is hitting that trail on a regular basis and embedding the path deep into his brain, while the old path, "over the hills and through the woods," is becoming overgrown and barely noticeable by his brain.

Something else has happened in the user's brain. It has become desensitized with excessive and repeated porn use. The brain has actually been over-stimulated from the flood of chemicals produced in the process, so it has to shut down some receptors to protect itself. By now, regular porn use has become more of an addiction that needs to be fed. The brain wants its hit, but now that the receptors have been shut down, it needs a bigger hit to get the same high. Which means it needs more, new, and different. Internet porn provides a ready supply of more, new, and different. This explains the progressive change in the brain. With more use, needs eventually escalate to crazier, harder porn in order to get the brain its hit. When that isn't enough, the user may branch out to live chat.

In more extreme cases, even the variety of internet porn or live chat doesn't satisfy anymore, so the user needs to take "variety" to another level by hooking up with live, in-the-flesh partners. Even this isn't about sex, it is about the brain getting its hit. At this point, the brain doesn't differentiate between porn and sex; it needs "new and different" to get its fix. Don't freak out yet. Not every husband's addiction reaches this level. I include this information for your awareness.

Desensitization is why your husband loses interest in having sex with you. It doesn't have anything to do with the way you look, how you perform, or how much he loves you. Normal doesn't arouse his brain anymore because it has been desensitized to normal sex. Porn has hijacked his brain. It is at this point that you will begin to notice sexual performance changes in your husband, like him having a hard time reaching climax (no, he doesn't suddenly have increased stamina—he just can't reach an orgasm via normal, healthy sex), or erectile dysfunction. Yep. You've been P.I.E.D: Porn-Induced Erectile Dysfunction.

Porn addiction will cause other changes in your husband as well. You might notice he isn't really present during sex. Or he might start using harsher language and asking you to perform sex acts with which you are uncomfortable. Most likely, you'll notice he is very selfish in the sack, and you feel like you are nothing more than an object for his pleasure. Your pleasure isn't even a blip on his radar. There is no longer intimacy between you.

This is what happens when the short cut to ecstasy has been traveled so often that it cuts a deep pathway in the brain. Repetition has created neural pathways for porn use that override the pathway for "over the hills and through the woods" kind of sex. Also, the *go/stop* system has gone haywire. The *go* system no longer waits for permission from the *stop* system. This is one explanation for why porn addicts can sit at a computer for hours on end jerking off to porn. The addict is completely consumed by the brain's desire to *go*.

Another side effect of porn addiction is sensitization. The addict's brain actually becomes hypersensitive to arousal cues. This could include people in everyday life, boobs, butts, inanimate objects, clothing, and normal, everyday situations with even the slightest sexual charge to them. Habitual use of porn has made the user's brain so sensitized that it sees sexual cues everywhere, making sexual fantasizing difficult to resist. This adds to the feeding of the addiction.

Porn addiction affects the user on an emotional level as well. Little by little, he changes. He becomes cold and detached. His moods may be erratic. He blows up at the smallest things, and he may be more combative. Then, after getting into an argument with his wife, he feels entitled to go use. Spending time with you and the kids or friends doesn't interest him as much. His motivation levels may decrease. He isn't getting as much done because all he can think about is making time to use porn. He also may be taking more risks and using in places where he might be found out. He could be spending money on porn and causing financial hardship in the family. Many porn addicts use at work, which could lead to him losing his job. These consequences are common to all drug addicts.

Your husband could be doing any or all of these things, depending on how deep he has fallen into addiction. And it's devastating. I understand the loss you are feeling right now. You are riddled with emotions of love, hate, anger, rage, sadness, depression, and anxiety. All these feelings are swirling around in your head at the same time, leaving you to feel the life has been sucked out of you. It is difficult to find anyone to talk to because no one will understand what you are going through if they haven't experienced it themselves. You might hear some people say, "What's the big deal?" And you're thinking, "I'll tell you what the big fricking deal is; my life has just been blown apart." Your husband's porn addiction has left you feeling hopeless and powerless and I'll bet you feel like your life will never be the same.

This discovery has created a plethora of emotions for you. Give yourself permission to feel it all. You have every right to feel betrayed, cheated on, and lost. If it helps you for now, go to bed and hide under the covers if that feels right. If you can't function at work, call in sick. If you need to call a therapist, you make that call. If you need to go see your doctor, call and tell them you need to get in ASAP. You do whatever you have to do to get through these first few days post-discovery.

I want you to keep in mind that eventually you will need to pick yourself up and face your future. Don't get stuck in your pain. It will serve you to move forward as soon as you can, even if it is just one turtle step at time. Trust me. I have been where you are right now, and I want you to know that you are not alone. I understand your pain.

His addiction does not have to break you. You will be ok. You will get your life back, and I am going to show you the way.

CHAPTER 3:

Should I Stay or Should I Go?

This is the burning question and you probably want the answer right now. Slow down. You don't need to have that answer this red-hot minute. You will get that figured out in good time. There is a way to work through this so you can make that decision from a clear head. Now is not the time to make a decision based on a knee-jerk reaction. You are probably very emotional, and that is rarely the state of mind from which you should be making life-changing decisions. Stick with me. I will show you how to get there.

Confronting His Addiction Head-On

The experts often recommend that you approach your husband calmly with a plan of how you will confront him, and I agree that this is the best course of action. If you are able to confront your husband in a calm, well-thought-out manner, that's awesome. But it doesn't always go down like that.

Discovery doesn't always come wrapped neatly with a tidy bow. In my case, I was blindsided by the discovery that my husband had a secret porn addiction, and, worse, I found out while he was standing right in front of me. There was no time to process and formulate a plan. I was too busy reacting to the news that he had been having sex with his virtual porn stars for over a year. All that time he'd been telling me he wasn't cheating on me, he actually had been. I wasn't crazy!

I didn't have time to catch my breath, say a mantra, or meditate in order to regain my "sense of calm." In that moment, there was no way to have a plan and there was no way I was going to let this discovery go one minute without being addressed. Instead, I went bat-s crazy on him. Do I wish it had happened differently? At this point, it doesn't matter. It happened like it did.

Many women experience trauma when they first discover their husband's porn or sex addiction. Professional therapists say wives suffer many of the same symptoms associated with Post Traumatic Stress Disorder after discovering their husband's porn addiction. There is also the possibility that discovery will trigger past traumas. If this is the case for you, schedule an appointment with your therapist right away. You will need additional support if you suffer from PTSD—or any unresolved, past trauma for that matter.

I'm throwing out a word of caution. If circumstances mean that you have no choice but to confront your husband in the heated moment of discovery, just make sure there are no blunt objects, knives, guns or other weapons of mass destruction at hand. You are in deep pain, and I know you want him to feel that pain, too. I can't condone physical violence of any kind, even though I can totally relate to the urge!

Be prepared for things not to go super-well. The reality is, when you confront him, he is probably not going to get it. Like any addict, he is going to be in denial that there is a problem, and he probably won't be able to see how this hurts you.

Remember how science shows the addict is desensitized and begins to see women as objects? This is the real-life evidence of that fact. He truly believes this does not affect you. His brain has been hijacked. That said, somewhere in him, he does feel shame—and he may very well defend himself against that feeling by telling you that *you* are the one with the problem. Don't buy into it. You did not cause this!

The discovery confrontation is tricky. If you find out with your husband right there with you, you just have to go with what comes up for you. But if you're alone when you discover your husband's porn addiction, resist the urge to search him out and fly off the handle. Give yourself enough time to pull yourself together, but not so much time that you begin to avoid the problem. You can be just as assertive from a calm state of mind as you can from a state of rage. If you think it would be safer to confront him with a third party present, call on a professional to help.

This confrontation is not necessarily the time when you are going to get everything figured out. This is the time to let him know that you are aware of his problem, that you are very hurt by his behavior, and that he has to stop using. He will most likely be stunned by your discovery and will probably be on the defensive. I have learned that when someone is in defense mode, they aren't really hearing you. I suggest you be prepared to have two separate conversations. The first conversation is the discovery conversation, which we are talking about now. After you have both had a few days to process the discovery, it will be time to have the second conversation, which I call the transparent conversation. This is when you may want to ask more probing questions as to the extent of his use and when you will be setting firm boundaries. I will talk more about the transparent conversation later in this chapter. For now, let's look at the discovery conversation.

When confronting your husband, it would serve you to avoid attacking him or shaming him. Focus on his behavior, not his character. Clearly communicate how his behavior makes you feel and that you expect him to stop.

Your husband may react in a number of different ways. He may try to shift the focus to your behavior for having violated his privacy. Let him know you are willing to talk about that later, but for now, keep the focus on his behavior. He also may try to minimize his problem, or claim he is entitled to use. He may try to blame you for his porn use. Again, calmly bring him back to his behavior. He may whine like a baby and claim he needs his porn because he is so stressed out. Firmly hold him accountable for choosing to handle his stress in an unhealthy way. Don't allow his manipulation attempts to sway you from the issue at hand. "You are addicted to porn. Our relationship is suffering because of it. I feel betrayed. You have to stop." Then set a time for the Transparent Conversation.

No matter how he reacts to being confronted, stand firm and stay focused. It will serve you to remain in control of the situation without escalating emotions. If he threatens your safety in any way, call the police. It is of utmost importance that you take every precaution to ensure your safety.

Caution: if there is any history of physical abuse in your relationship, I definitely recommend you seek the help of a therapist in mediating the confrontation. It would be best for you to find a therapist who specializes in sexual addiction. Let me be clear. Not a sex therapist, but a sex *addiction* therapist.

****

The confrontation is now behind you. Whether you got here via a calm, planned confrontation or by way of Hiroshima, it is time to take the next step. Before we move on, I am going to ask you to consider one thing. Please, just consider this idea: *Your husband is not the enemy. His porn addiction is the enemy.*

I understand this might be a hard pill to swallow at this point. I'm not asking you to buy into it if you aren't ready. I'm just asking you to consider the possibility. If both of you can at least consider that porn is the enemy, you both might be open to fighting this addiction together. There is nothing better to bridge two opposing forces than to have a common enemy.

In the interim, it might be wise for you to get some distance from your husband so you can cool down. Take some time to yourself and cry it out. Get out of town for a day or two. Spoil yourself with self-care. Take a bath or go for a swim. Get out in nature. Sleep if you can. If you have a journal, write in it. If you don't have a journal, buy one. Your thoughts are swirling around in your head like a stage four tornado. Get them out of your head and onto paper so you can get some relief. Whenever your thoughts start to swirl again, write them down. You may have a lot of questions about your husband's porn use, so write those down, too. This is part of your healing process. Give yourself the time and space you need to get your bearings before moving forward.

If you feel the need to talk with someone I am going to caution you to carefully choose with whom you share in the beginning. You are feeling raw and very vulnerable right now. You will need someone you can trust to be neutral, compassionate, and understanding. Someone who will give you space to feel your feelings without judging you or your husband. Steer clear of anyone who might counsel you from a place of shame. In many cases, pastors or clergy members have actually done more harm than good. Shame is destructive and will not serve you through this healing process. I suggest you find a trusted friend, therapist, or coach.

You may be tempted to run for a vice of your own to numb your pain. Don't do it. Numbing yourself may compound your problems. When you self-medicate as a way of dealing with your pain, you are only suppressing it temporarily. Your painful feelings won't vanish. They will be there waiting for you as soon as you sober up.

Some of us are adept at blocking our pain through avoidance. This might be ok for a while, but eventually those painful feelings will resurface. Wouldn't you rather control when and how that happens, instead of waiting for them to surface at the most inappropriate time when you are in a situation where you don't want others to see you in total meltdown? One way or another, you will eventually have to deal with your painful feelings.

The only way out of pain is through it. Face your feelings straight on and allow them to surface. As best you can, allow yourself to feel whatever you are feeling. Pay attention to your emotions and identify exactly what it is you are feeling: sadness, rage, grief, hate. Scan your body, notice where you feel the emotion, and give it a physical description.

It might sound like this: *This grief feels like a tight knot in my stomach and I feel nauseated,* or *I feel the sadness in my chest, it feels tight and closed off.* You get the idea? Resisting your feelings may increase their intensity. Allow your feelings to flow through you so you can release them. Cue up a playlist of your favorite "love gone wrong" songs and have a cry fest. This is how you take control of your feelings rather than allowing your feelings to control you.

Don't beat yourself up for being intensely emotional. You can only do your best. In some cases, women are so distraught and consumed by anxiety or depression that they need to see their physician to discuss medication as an interim solution until they are functioning normally again. If you think this would serve you, call your doctor right away.

It is so important that you take care of yourself at this time. You need time to catch your breath before taking the next step. You don't have to figure it all out right at this very minute. Slow down and take your time. This is a process.

Rebuilding trust through transparent conversation

As defined by Merriam-Webster, *trust* is "the assured reliance on the character, ability, strength, or truth of someone or something."

Your trust has been demolished. You may be feeling you can never trust him again. I felt the same way. Your husband has a lot to answer for, and he is going to have to work hard to regain your trust. And there will be plenty of work to do on your part as well. You will have to ask some difficult questions and be prepared to hear difficult answers.

Now that you have gained your bearings after your discovery conversation, it is time you prepare yourself for the transparent conversation with your husband. If possible, choose a time and place where you both can be relaxed and open. When I had this conversation with my husband, I chose my "place of peace" on the shores of Lake Michigan. For me, the energy of the water is very healing, and being there helped me stay calm. Where do you find your place of peace? This is a very important conversation; so choose a place where you will both feel safe.

Your mind has been preoccupied with thoughts about his porn use, and that's understandably left you with many questions. How long has he been using? When did it start? How often? When does he use? Does he use it at work? Was he using it that time he didn't answer my call? How many times did he lie to me so that he could use? Are our kids at risk? What kind of porn turns him on? Is he into hard-core porn? Has he had sex with another person? Do I need to be tested for STDs? These are just some examples of the tough questions you may want answers to in order to find peace of mind. If he is going to regain your trust, he needs to start by being completely transparent in answering all your questions.

Your husband is going to feel quite uncomfortable with your questions and in hearing your pain. That isn't your problem. While the truth is often difficult to hear, the truth is easier to deal with than lies. There have been enough lies already. This will be a vulnerable conversation for you both. His honesty is just as important for his own recovery as it is for yours.

At this time, your husband may not be able to or feel safe enough to answer all your questions with absolute honesty. But as he goes through recovery, he will learn that honesty is an integral part of true intimacy. For many men, most of their problem is that they don't know how to express their physical or emotional needs. They will learn this, too, in recovery.

Your husband will need to be prepared to do some deep listening as you express your feelings and he needs to be open to answering your questions. You will need to be assertive in this conversation. Prepare your husband ahead of time. Let him know you expect his open and honest answers to your questions, and that you will do your best to hold a safe space for him to do so. His defensiveness or evasiveness will defeat the effectiveness of this conversation. That said, he caused this problem, and his transparency will be his first steps in fixing it.

This conversation is for you. This is your time to be heard, to ask your questions, and to provide your husband with a road map for regaining your trust. He needs to acknowledge your pain and frustration. He has to try to see things through your eyes. Have your questions prepared and your boundaries clearly defined.

Your husband will most likely not want to initiate this conversation, so you will probably be the one in the driver seat. Don't be passive. You have the questions that need to be answered and you will be spelling out your boundaries, so it makes sense that you take charge.

During this conversation, you can be assertive–but resist the temptation to be aggressive. Avoid sarcasm, contempt, criticism, blame, or statements starting with "you never" or "you always." It will not serve either of you if he is on the defensive. Stick with "I" statements as much as possible. "I feel _______" instead of "You make me feel _______." This helps to avoid blaming, shaming, and judgment, which might shut down the conversation before it gets started.

Communication is key. The way you communicate will determine the success or failure of this transparent conversation. Communication has the word "commune" in it. It is about bringing parties together. While you will want to be assertive, it is important to remember that *you* matter, and that *he* matters too. You will need to provide an open and compassionate space for him to be honest and vulnerable. He will need to hold that same compassionate space for you, as some of his honest answers are going to hurt. This conversation, if held in mutual respect and compassion, will be the first step in regaining trust and in bringing you together to fight the enemy of porn addiction.

Setting Boundaries

Boundaries are not a form of punishment. They are a necessary step in rebuilding trust. You are actually showing your love for him by setting boundaries. These boundaries will establish a clear road map for your husband to follow in regaining your trust. With clear boundaries in place, you can do your work and he can do his work.

For many of us, setting boundaries is a new concept, and you may find it difficult to know where to begin. The most important consideration when setting boundaries is knowing what you can and can't control. You will want to focus your energy on things that will make a difference for you feeling safe in the relationship and for a successful recovery for him.

In setting boundaries, consider what will make you feel safe. Do you need him to move into the guest room or maybe even move out of the house temporarily? Do you need to get away? It will serve you to look at the things that bother you most. If you need help in setting boundaries, it's a great idea to consult a therapist or coach. Many of the boundaries you set will depend on the severity and nature of your husband's porn use. In my experience, there are a few "non-negotiable" boundaries that must be adhered to if you are going to have any chance of rebuilding your relationship.

1. No porn!! Zero tolerance.
2. He finds and installs porn software protection on "all" devices. There are several programs and apps that will send a report to an accountability partner, which will list visits to any questionable sites.
3. He enrolls in and regularly attends a recovery program for porn/ sex addiction.
4. He enrolls in individual counseling with a professional trained in porn/sex addiction and must attend on a regular basis.
5. 90 days of abstinence. No masturbation or sex with spouse. Many recovery programs will cover this, but it is good for you to have in place regardless. In *Covenant Eyes, The Porn Circuit*, sex addiction expert Dr. Mark Laaser recommends abstinence to help your husband learn that he won't die without sex. He also needs this time to rebuild intimacy with you. The old pathway, "over the hills and through the woods," needs to be re-established.
6. If there has been extramarital sex, you both need to be tested for STDs.

Your husband may be a bit resistant to these boundaries. And that is ok. As long as he is willing to try, this effort is enough to start. My husband didn't think he needed these boundaries at first, but he later changed his mind.

In my husband's own words: "In the beginning, I thought I could break this addiction on my own as I had when I quit smoking cigarettes, but I realized porn addiction was too powerful for me to beat it on my own. I needed my wife to set these clear boundaries for me because I probably wouldn't have set them for myself. These boundaries were my start to recovery. The benefits of being in a program have made the road to my recovery much faster. Looking back, I can now see how pornography negatively impacted my life and relationships. Porn was controlling many aspects of my life. I am healing and my relationships are healing because I accepted my wife's boundaries and enrolled in a recovery program."

Some husbands may need more convincing than others that a recovery program is the right route to take. Others may not be convinced they are addicted to porn. If your husband needs convincing, here's more from my husband's sex addiction therapist. Tom Shelder:

> It is extremely important for men... to seek specialized professional help. The goal of porn addiction recovery is to abstain from porn use while relearning how to have an intimate relationship involving sex. Treating porn addiction is a delicate, difficult, and long-term process. The porn addict needs to engage in honest self-reflection to determine what, why, and how this addiction needs to be fueled. He needs to determine the source of the pain that he is attempting to mask or escape from. Then he must work through the treatment process to learn what true intimacy is and differentiate the sexual act from it. Only a therapist who is specifically trained in the complexities of sexual addiction can effectively take this client through this complex and long-term process.
>
> The individual who begins sexual addiction therapy will be evaluated in order to find a starting point for his individual treatment. Then he will go through basic steps similar to a 12-step program but designed with the intricacies and uniqueness of sexual addiction. There is often homework for the client

to complete each week, accountability partners and group therapies are usually part of the process. As the addict goes through this process, he sees he is not alone, that he can change his behaviors and desires and he can learn what true intimacy is, as well as how fulfilling the sexual relationship can be.

Upon discovering her husband's addictive behavior, the wife must first realize that there is help available. She must also try to understand that this is an addiction, similar to other addictions, and it will take hard emotional work and time, a lifetime perhaps. There will be things that they will need to agree on that the wife will and should hold her husband accountable to, such as her having open access to all phone and computers; television and internet viewing; and of course, accountability to the whereabouts of the addict. There may be disclosures of the addict's behaviors and extramarital affairs and the wife will need to be prepared for these difficult disclosures. The open disclosures are a very important part of the addict's recovery. Divorce often becomes part of the discussion during the therapy process; therefore, the wife will need to be committed and prepared for difficult conversations. The wife of a porn/ sex addict will have a significant role in his recovery. With commitment and patience, it can be extremely gratifying and can create a more beautiful and intimate, committed relationship during this process.

I feel very lucky that my husband chose to stop using pornography. The only problem was that he believed that with willpower he could fight the addiction on his own. This strategy worked for about nine months. Then he found himself sucked into using again, which lead to seven months of deception and secrecy. I have read somewhere that it is easier to quit cocaine than it is to quit porn. I'll write more about my husband's relapse in coming chapters.

Ultimately, the choice to abandon pornography is your husband's to make. The only way to break an unhealthy habit is to want something else more. It won't serve him to choose recovery only to save your relationship or to make you happy. He must make the choicc because he wants to be healthy more than he wants to use drugs. This has to be for him. It is the only way he will be successful at recovery.

There are also a few boundaries you can set for yourself. Some women feel a compelling need to be intimate with their husband during the first days after discovery. It seems to come from a place of proving something. Either she needs to feel her husband still loves her, or that he is attracted to her, to feel that safe connection she fears is gone forever. In any case, she runs the risk of being disappointed, which could make her feel worse about herself. If you find yourself in this situation, proceed with caution.

It might serve you to set your own boundary for sexual intimacy. You need time and space to heal yourself. This may be a scary boundary to set because you may fear it may drive him to use porn. This is not your business. You do not need to be the porn police. He needs to police himself no matter the stress he might be under. If he should decide to use porn because you set this boundary, consider it valuable feedback. Also, I strongly recommend you set the boundary to not rescue him from the consequences of his actions. No excuse-making or covering up for him. No "letting him slide" on boundary enforcement because he's "under stress." Let him face the music for his choices.

One of the most important boundaries you can set for yourself is to allow him to work his own program. On one hand, you need to be aware that he is following through with his program, as this will demonstrate his commitment to recovery. This information will give you valuable feedback in determining whether to stay in the relationship or not. On the other hand, you cannot be policing his attendance or his progress. That is all up to him.

Your Recovery Program

This is your opportunity to work on you. Not because you caused his porn addiction or because it will help him through his recovery, but because it will help you become a stronger person no matter what he does. Once he is in a program, it is no longer your business as to how he works it. Your business is to take care of yourself. You need your own program to keep yourself on track.

One of the easiest traps to get caught in when you have an addict in your life is to fall into a pattern of co-dependent like behaviors. The definition of co-dependent as described by author Melody Beattie in *Codependent No More* is "a person who has let another person's behavior affect him or her, and who is obsessed with controlling that person's behavior."

Because you have been traumatized and you desperately want to feel safe again, you may be tempted to work his program for him, to babysit him, or to police his success and failures. It will not serve you to obsess, to control, or to worry about his behavior 24/7. You might think these tactics will bring you peace of mind, but this couldn't be farther from the truth. Trying to control someone else will drive you crazy.

Another behavior that might show up in this situation is you wanting to help your husband in ways that don't actually help him–like enabling his negative behaviors by making excuses for him and protecting him from the consequences of his actions. Enabling only allows him to stay sick. Your husband needs to experience his consequences and needs to be held accountable.

It will be tempting to put your own needs aside for your husband's and you may have a difficult time saying no to him; but, there will be times when a *no* to him is a *yes* to you. Because you believe you will feel safer if he gets better, you will be tempted to put too much of your energy into his healing while neglecting your own healing.

You may believe that your happiness is dependent upon what *he* does or doesn't do. Your sense of well-being may be so off kilter that you find your reactions to circumstances to be out of proportion by either over reacting or under-reacting The irony of all these co-dependent like behaviors is that they are actually a self-destructive response to someone else's destructive behavior.

The best reason for working your own program is to heal your wounds. If you don't truly heal from this trauma it will affect all your current and future relationships. If both you and your husband work on your own healing, your relationship could become better than ever. Or, say you decided to leave this relationship without working your own program. You will later find yourself in the same kind of relationship with a different guy.

I see relationships as assignments from the Universe bringing you lessons for your soul's growth. If you don't learn the lessons now, you will attract another relationship that may show up looking different initially, but will be delivering the same lessons. Have you ever had a friend who time and time again lands in a dysfunctional relationship, and then when the relationship ends she always asks, "Why do I always attract this kind of guy?" She thinks she is a victim of circumstance, but she is creating her own problems because she hasn't done her own work. She needs to heal her wounds in order to attract someone different.

You need support right now. As your husband needs support for his recovery, you need support for yours. Don't make the mistake of thinking, "If he just quits, our life will go back to normal."

Working your own program will give you clarity and strength, which will empower you to make the decisions you need to make regarding your life and your relationship. Had I not been working my own program, I would not have gained this sense of independence and conviction for choosing who and what I want in my life. I have taken my life back.

There is a chance that your husband will remain in denial about his addiction, and he might decide that he doesn't need a recovery program nor does he need to stop his behavior. While this may leave you feeling hopeless and helpless, I am going to say, "Pick yourself up, shake off the dust, and get to work on your own recovery." His choices will provide you information and valuable feedback about his commitment to your relationship. Hang in there and do your own work because you will make better decisions from a place of strength rather than from a place of weakness. As you get further into your recovery, you will become clearer about whether you should stay or go.

CHAPTER 4:

Surrender and Your Spiritual Practice

"God,
Grant me the Serenity to accept the things I cannot change;
The Courage to change the things I can;
And the Wisdom to know the difference"

I want you to give yourself a pat on the back. You have made it through some of the most difficult steps on the way to your recovery. You have made it through discovery and through the very difficult transparency conversation with your husband. You have asked difficult questions and you have accepted the uncomfortable answers. You have been fearless in setting boundaries and in laying your husband's roadmap back to regaining your trust. Now it is time to focus on you.

His addiction has brought you to your knees, and the world you knew is gone. You are feeling weak, hopeless, and powerless. It is very normal for you to feel this way. Now is the perfect time for the next step. I'm about to say something that may sound counterintuitive, but keep an open mind. By accepting that you are powerless over him and his addiction, you are going to find your own power.

You cannot control your husband's addiction. The only thing you can do is to surrender it. You have to "Let Go and Let God." It will be so tempting to try and control his porn addiction and even his recovery. It is common to think, "If he stops using porn, I will be happy." With this thought in mind, you will do everything you can to make sure he stops. You will tie yourself into knots trying to make sure he doesn't use porn. You will try every trick in the book from getting angry, to crying, to manipulating, and you might even throw out the guilt-laden statement, "If you love me, you will quit." None of that will work. You have to realize that right now, not even he is in control of his porn addiction–so what on earth makes you think you can control it?

We feel out of control because we want to manage and control the addict and his behavior. But when you put all your energy into controlling him, your own life goes to hell because you aren't putting any energy into managing you. You spend your time policing him and you neglect your own self-care. Nothing you do or don't do is going to stop him from using, nor is it going to change him in any way. Trying to control his porn addiction is going to drive you insane. But you can choose another way.

You must stop the struggle. Release the need to control him and admit you are powerless over his porn addiction. You are powerless to change him. The only person you have any power over is YOU. The only person you can control or change is YOU. It is your responsibility to take care of yourself. Let your husband take care of himself. When you take care of you, you will find that your happiness no longer depends on what he does or doesn't do. You will regain your peace of mind when you focus on your own life.

This isn't going to happen overnight. This is all part of the recovery process that happens one day at a time. And sometimes, it is going to be hour-by-hour, or even minute-by-minute. You will have good days and bad days. You might be sailing along having a great day when something happens and steals your bliss. Your mood will change, and you will be stuck in pain again. One minute you will be feeling sane, and the next you are feeling like you are spinning out of control. In those moments I want you to remember the Serenity Prayer. This simple but powerful prayer will help restore your sanity.

This is the point where I bring in spirituality. When I talk about God, I am not speaking of religious dogma. I use the term God in the sense of a Universal force that is omnipresent. You can choose to use the term Higher Power, Creator, Spirit, Universe, Force, Allah, Shiva, Krishna, Angels, or anything else–it doesn't matter to me. The point is that you can rely on a power greater than yourself to get you through this difficult time. Traditional 12-step programs use the terms God or Higher Power, as will I. With that said, I would like to teach you the Serenity Prayer, as used by Al-Anon. It has brought me peace of mind in the most difficult of times.

"God, grant me the serenity to accept the things I cannot change." Accept that you can't change your husband, his addiction, your co-workers, or your family members. You cannot change circumstances. You can't change anyone or anything any more than you can change the weather. Oh, sometimes we all get stuck in thinking we can, then we struggle and resist until we are exhausted from trying. We make ourselves crazy trying to change things that are out of our control because we believe the lie that we can. But we don't have to spend our energy on all this crazy-making activity. We can choose to surrender all of it to God.

"God, grant me the courage to change the things I can." This brings it back to you and the truth that the only thing you can change is you. When you start to live this truth, you will realize that your happiness does not come from outside yourself; your happiness comes from within you. Happiness is an inside job.

Where have you put someone else's needs in front of your own? When have you said yes to someone else in order to please them when you really wanted to say no? Where have you looked for approval and validation from others? Where have you sought love from someone else that you should have given to yourself? If you can find the places in your life where you did any or all of these things, I am willing to bet you are suffering because of it. These are the things you may want to change for yourself.

We all get caught up in seeking love, appreciation, and approval from others, because we are looking for them to show us our value and our worth. We turn ourselves inside out and upside-down in order to receive this validation. But here is the problem with this behavior. When we look outside ourselves for our value and our worth, we are never satisfied. Our thirst for love and approval is never quenched. Have you ever had someone tell you they love you, but in your mind you think, "Yes, but if you really loved me you would ______"? Or someone tell you that you are beautiful and you think, "Yes, but you are just saying that"? We all do it.

The only thing you can change is you, and the best place to start is in changing the way you treat yourself. Start giving yourself all the things you are expecting others to give you. Change the way you think about yourself. Change the way you show up in the world. Take your own advice. Use all that brilliant advice you so willingly share with others about how they should change their lives and use it to change your own life! Be courageous and change YOU!

"God, grant me the wisdom to know the difference." There is a way I like to reword this for my personal use: "God, remind me to tap into my inner wisdom that knows the difference." You don't have to study anything, acquire any additional knowledge, or be granted this wisdom. It is already within you! Your body is tuned in to your inner wisdom. Your body rebels when you believe the lie that you can change circumstances outside your control. Your body feels grounded when you are standing in your truth of what you can change.

I am going to teach you how to tap into your inner wisdom, which is the part of you I call the Higher Self with a capital "S." This Self is the part of you that is in the likeness of and is directly connected to the Divine Creator, which I call God. This is the part of you that has all the answers you seek. Your Higher Self knows exactly how to get you through this crisis, and when you tap into this inner guidance, you will find your way to taking back your life. This is where your peace is.

Hearing this, you might be asking, "If this Self is part of me, then why don't I tap into its guidance more often?" The short answer is that you have been conditioned to tune it out because the negative voice of fear in your head always speaks loudest and first.

Think about it. Right now, how many of your thoughts are consumed with fear? Fear for your future, fear that your husband doesn't love you, fear that you are not going to be ok, fear that because he is addicted to porn there is something wrong with you. I have a hunch that your list of fear thoughts goes on and on. You are not alone. This is the part of your mind that runs on what I call the negative script. This is the part of you that is driven by fear and that drives your decisions based on society's beliefs. This script was developed when we were small children and took on the beliefs of others. Some fear is good, because it keeps you safe in the eye of imminent danger. But the negative script often keeps you from listening to your Higher Self by clouding your mind with unwarranted fears.

You will know which voice you are listening to when you check into your body to see how it feels. It is that simple. Your body will tell you when you believe the lies of the negative script vs. listening to the truth of your Higher Self.

Be careful what you believe. Have you ever noticed the word believe has "lie" in the middle of it? Personally, I am careful not to use the word belief, because beliefs are usually given to us from someone else. We are conditioned to believe something so that we are socially acceptable. I like to use the word "know" instead of believe whenever possible, because it refers to the internal wisdom and truth of my Higher Self.

With this knowledge about your inner wisdom, you are ready to calibrate your Inner Guidance Meter. See the diagram below. -10 represents the worst you could feel, zero is neutral, and +10 represents the best you can feel.

Inner Guidance Meter

Fear Peace

I--0--I

-10 +10

First, I want you to take yourself back to a moment in time that was a negative experience, a time when fear had a tight grip on you. Close your eyes, breath deep, take yourself back to that moment in time, and allow yourself to experience the event with all your senses. Let the experience fill every cell in your body, flowing from the top of your head to the tips of your toes. Now scan your body; notice the physical sensations, where in your body you feel them and give them a physical description. Start with your feet and work your way up to your neck, face and head. While you are in that feeling state I want you to give it a number from -10 to +10. Write that number down. Going forward, when you experience this negative feeling state in your body, this is a cue that you believe something that isn't true for you and therefore you are reacting from fear. Now, shake off that negative feeling and take a couple of deep, cleansing breaths.

This time I want you to do the same thing—except, take yourself back to a moment in time when you felt completely at peace and happy. Repeat all the previous steps, and give this feeling state a number from -10 to +10. Going forward, when you experience this positive feeling state in your body, this is a cue that you are living your truth and therefore responding from peace. Notice that in the negative numbers you are *reacting* in fear, and in the positive numbers you are *responding* in peace.

As you recover from the trauma of your husband's porn addiction, you may find yourself bouncing back and forth from fear to peace—and there may be times when you are stuck in the fear state. In later chapters, I will teach you powerful tools to help you shift from fear to peace. For now, I want you to start with the awareness of the fearful thoughts that are preceding your negative feeling state. Be curious. Ask yourself, "What am I afraid of right in this moment?" I want you to write those thoughts down in your journal. They will be useful to you later in your recovery process.

When you find yourself in the fear state, you can restore yourself to peace by reciting the Serenity Prayer. This will remind you that you are powerless over your husband's porn addiction, and it will bring you to a state of surrender. If you have to, repeat it over and over until you feel even the smallest shift toward positive numbers on your Inner Guidance Meter. Don't worry if you aren't moving from -7 to +5. Even one step from -7 to -6 is progress. Use your Guidance Meter to track your progress in the moment. Let your Higher Self guide you toward peace. Your recovery process is about progress, not perfection.

Now is the time to surrender your will to a power greater than yourself, as they say in Al-Anon, a power that can restore you to sanity. You don't have to do this alone. You can lean on Spirit to shore you up and see you through. Your Higher Self is your direct connection to Spirit. Have faith in this omnipresent force from which you were created, for this is where you will find your strength. "His Strength not Mine" would be a powerful mantra to use when you are feeling like you can't make it through a tough time.

Many religious leaders do more harm than good to both addicts and wives by addressing this problem from a position of shame. Because of this, my inner wisdom tells me that while religion does not have a role in my recovery, God certainly does. If you don't already have a strong connection to your Higher Power, you may find it difficult at first to have faith in something you can't see. This is where your spiritual practice will come into play. Faith is like a muscle you have to build and strengthen. With repeated exercise, your faith will grow stronger and stronger. The more often you surrender to and trust in your Higher Power, the stronger your connection will grow. You have to spend consistent, dedicated time developing faith in your Higher Power.

An important note: Spirit will not intervene without an invitation. You have to call upon Him and surrender yourself to His will. So if you find yourself in a painful situation, call on Him. The same applies for Angels, Saints, Ascended Masters, or any other form of Divine Intervention. They have to be invited if you want their help.

What is a spiritual practice? Spiritual practice varies from person to person, and as we grow and evolve, so does our practice. For some it may be study of religious text. For others it may be meditation and/or prayer. My practice has evolved over the years. While my personal relationship with God has always been my foundation, I have tried many different spiritual practices. Twenty-some years ago, I started with Angels and Al-Anon. I've also dabbled in the Native American tradition of Animal Medicine, Eastern Religion, and even Numerology. All of which connect me to the Divine wisdom that resides within me. Now I practice *A Course in Miracles*, which is a psycho-spiritual mind retraining that teaches universal spiritual truths to shift yourself from a state of fear to love.

You have to find what resonates with you. Have fun and explore a variety of spiritual paths until you find the one that feels a good fit for you. You don't have to have a fancy ritual to connect with your Higher Power. He is always there waiting for you to call. Your practice could be as simple as sitting down in a quiet place and having a conversation with your Higher Power. Whatever practices you choose; practice every day, preferably first thing in the morning. Just five minutes spent with God, first thing in the morning, has the power to change the course of your entire day. A short and powerful prayer that I like to start my day with is:

Dear God,
I surrender myself to you, that your will be mine.
May I see as you see, hear as you hear, speak of your word,
breathe of your breath,
and walk in your steps. May I do as You would have me do.
And so it is. Amen

Keep in mind that your circumstances may not miraculously change, but with the help of your Higher Power, your perceptions will change, and this will change your experience. Miracles happen every day. A miracle is as simple as a change in your perception. This is something you do have control over. All you have to do is invite God in, surrender yourself and the situation to Him, offer your willingness to see things differently and He will help you create miracles in your life.

I will share with you one of my favorite prayers by author, speaker, and spiritual teacher, Marianne Williamson.

Dear God,
Be in me. May my thoughts be your thoughts.
Take this situation that I have called to mind for I know my
pain derives from circumstances that are kept, at least in part,
in place by my thinking. And so I pray dear God for help.
I am willing to see things differently. Please work a miracle

within my mind that I might be free of pain.
And so it is. Amen

Over the years, my spiritual practice has saved me from my suffering more times than I can list–especially in these past three years since the initial discovery of my husband's porn addiction. The first year after discovery, I wasn't committed to a daily spiritual practice. I would do it as needed in the heat of a mini-crisis, but I didn't practice every day. I believed that I would be ok as long as my husband stopped using porn. I was wrong. Upon discovering his relapse, I realized the only way I was going to get through the devastation of his betrayal was to work my own recovery program and dedicate myself to a daily, spiritual practice. That decision truly changed my life because it changed me.

You have admitted you are powerless over your husband's porn addiction, and you have surrendered your will to your Higher Power that His strength will restore your life to a state of peace. You have your prayers and Guidance Meter tool to guide you. Now you are ready to do some heavy lifting and start cleaning up your life.

CHAPTER 5:

Cleaning Up Your Life

"Life is about relationships. The most important is your relationship with yourself. This relationship will determine the quality of every relationship in your life."
Sandy Brown

Why do I have to clean up my life when he is the one with the problem? Because the fastest way to release yourself from this pain is to own your own crap. You have to take responsibility for your part in your pain. It is easy to point your finger at your husband and believe that your happiness depends on his behavior. But what if he doesn't come through? Are you going to wait for him to save you? Hell, no. Your life depends on you. If you want to be free from this pain, you have to work on yourself.

Your freedom from pain is not going to come from anything he does or doesn't do. It will come from what *you* do or don't do. Doing your own work is the only way you will be set free from this pain. This may be difficult to accept right now, but stay with this process and you will discover this truth. If you are tired of suffering and want a way out of this pain, you have got to clean up your life.

It is time to start taking a fearless look at yourself: your strengths, your weaknesses, your fears, your desires, your patterns of self-sabotage, how you treat others, and your own addictions.

- ✓ Where are you not showing yourself the love you seek from others?
- ✓ Where are you not showing up for you?
- ✓ Where do you judge others?
- ✓ Where do you judge yourself?
- ✓ Where do you look to others to fill your needs?
- ✓ What substances have you used to escape your pain?
- ✓ What is your part in your pain?

You asked your husband to be totally honest with you: now it is time to be honest with yourself. To do this, you will need to dig deep and get dirty. It is time for you to grow, and you will need courage to see the things in yourself that you have not wanted to see.

This won't be a quick fix. Sometimes you will dive in with everything you have, and you might notice a lot of change in a short period of time. Other times, you may slip backward a bit, and that's ok because you needed to take a step back and dig a little deeper. Before you know it, you are moving forward again. Sometimes you will get lazy, and then you might feel stuck again. This is ok, too, because eventually you will wake up and start moving forward again. Stick with it and trust the process. Eventually you will come to see a beautiful version of yourself that you had no idea was in you.

"We don't have to improve ourselves; we just have to let go of what blocks our heart."
Jack Canfield

Recovery through self-discovery is not about "fixing" you. This process is about gaining an awareness of your negative behaviors so you can release the things that don't serve you. These behaviors are keeping you from the life you truly desire. Through awareness and acceptance, you will cultivate a love for yourself that no one else could ever give you. When you learn to meet your own needs and to love yourself, you will not have to depend on others to do it for you. You will be filling yourself with love from the inside out and as your vessel becomes full, love will spill out of you and onto others. You will no longer be focused on *getting* from others because you are so full that all you can do is *give* to others.

No more grasping to hold on to someone else's love or trying to force them to love you. You will be free to truly be yourself because you are no longer trying to be someone you are not in order to get love from others. From this state of being, you will attract people who love you as you are. This is freedom.

It is a mistake to believe that self-love is selfish, because when you have a healthy relationship with yourself, you will be in a position to choose healthier relationships. Your relationships with others, with money, with food, and with anything else will be healthier because you love yourself. Your strength comes from self-love. You will learn to celebrate your strengths and accept your weaknesses. When you can love yourself as you are, you will be able to love others as they are. Their actions will no longer have power over you because your power comes from within you. Again, this takes practice and will not happen overnight. Life won't stop kicking you in the ass. There are times you will still fall down, but each time you pick yourself up and practice self-love, you will grow stronger.

Change starts with awareness. In order to release the things that do not serve you, first you have to know what those things are. Turn off autopilot and wake the hell up! Observe your patterns, your fears, your thoughts, and your actions. No need to judge yourself, just notice and be present with what you are noticing. Become the self-observer.

The self-observer is standing on the outside looking in, calling the action play by play as a sports announcer calls a game. Look at your behaviors and your thoughts that caused those behaviors. This is the way to discover who you are and to learn acceptance for everything that you are. Being aware of your positive traits and your negative traits will allow you to be present with how you are showing up in any given moment. Because of this awareness, you will be able to release your painful, limiting beliefs, and self-sabotaging behaviors, while honoring all the positives in you. This is when miracles will happen and old wounds begin to heal.

You will cultivate self-awareness by being mindful of your actions. Little by little, you will become more aware of your negative, autopilot behaviors that brought you to painful circumstances. Where you once blamed others for your circumstances, you will take responsibility for yourself. At first, you will become aware of these behaviors through reflection after the fact. With practice, you will learn to "catch yourself in the act." Eventually, you will learn to avoid these negative, autopilot behaviors all together, and you won't find yourself in those negative circumstances any more. There is a poem by Portia Nelson called *There's a Hole in My Sidewalk: Autobiography in Five Short Chapters,* which I feel is a great description of what living your life from a place of acceptance and self-awareness looks like. I have paraphrased it below:

You are walking down the sidewalk and unexpectedly fall into a hole. You wonder, "How the hell did I get here?" You blame others for the hole being there and you struggle like hell to get out. Then, another day, you find yourself on that same sidewalk. This time you remember the hole is there, but you walk right into the hole anyway. You might take a little responsibility for having fallen in the hole because you knew better but you still think, "Darn it, why didn't someone fix this hole?" You struggle to get out of the hole, but it is little easier than the last time.

Once again you find yourself on that same sidewalk. You clearly see the hole, and you remember all the pain and struggle that the hole caused you. However, you think you can walk around it. You try this new approach only to fall in the hole again. But you waste no time blaming others for your predicament, and you take 100% responsibility for your choices. Climbing out of the hole is so much easier this time.

Another day comes and yet again you find yourself on this sidewalk. You clearly see the hole in front of you and, remembering all the times you fell in that very same hole, you stop yourself dead in your tracks. You say, "This time, I am going to take a different sidewalk."

As humans, if there is one thing we have in common it is that we all struggle with fear. As I said in the last chapter, there are times when fear is a good thing because it keeps us safe from harm. Other times, fear keeps us from the things we want most in our lives. It holds us back from following our dreams.

Fear often speaks loudest and first. This is often the voice we listen to when we are living on autopilot. It takes conscious effort to disconnect from the controlling voice of fear that I call my negative script. This script disconnects you from your Higher Self thereby disconnecting you from the fearless part of you, which is your truth. The negative script shows you limitations, whereas your Higher Self sees nothing but unlimited possibilities. I like this acronym for fear: False Evidence Appearing Real.

Have you ever found yourself dreaming of doing something that would bring you happiness and joy, something that feels full of possibility? When you envision yourself doing this, you have a feeling of "the sky is the limit." This is the way it feels when you have tapped into your truth. Your Higher Self is inspiring (in Spirit) you to do something that is in alignment with who you are meant to be.

This dream seems totally doable until, suddenly, your negative script chimes in to tell you all the reasons why it isn't possible for that dream to come true. "You aren't smart enough to do that." "You are too old to do that." "You won't be safe if you do that." These painful thoughts keep rolling in until the negative script has you stuck in fear and abandoning your dream.

The same thing could be happening right now. You may find yourself thinking that you love your husband deeply and you can see a glimpse of hope that the two of you can find your way through this, together. Thinking this brings you peace. This peaceful feeling is when you know you are connected to your Higher Self, because you are feeling hopeful, and in that moment, you are connected to Love. You are connected to your Higher Power, who is Love.

Then, the negative script pipes up. "He doesn't love you enough to stop using porn." "You can never trust him again." "He hurt you, so you have to leave him." "You're too _____, he doesn't want you." And there you are left feeling helpless, hopeless, confused, and stuck in fear.

On the other hand, you may find yourself thinking that your husband has gone too far, that he refuses to do anything about his addiction, and that you deserve better than this. You think you have to divorce him. Surprisingly, you find yourself feeling at peace with this scenario. Again, you are connected to your Higher Self. It honestly feels like this choice would bring you the most peace. You can feel it in your body, because your body feels relaxed.

Then, your negative script chimes in with all the fearful reasons why this won't work. "You will be alone the rest of your life if you leave him." "No one else will want you." "You can't make it on your own." "You will ruin your kids' lives if you leave him." And there you are left feeling helpless, hopeless, confused, and stuck in fear.

In both scenarios, you are paralyzed by fear and unable to take action. You are a balled up, confused mess. But, you don't have to be. I will teach you the tools to clear your fears and limiting beliefs, and from this of mind, you make decisions from a place of strength. With these to you will be able to recognize that the only thing standing in your way your own fearful thinking.

You have probably heard it before: "Change your thoughts to change your life." And you may have thought, "If it was that easy, I would have done it by now." While it is this simple, it might not be easy because it will take hard work on your part. But the more you work on your painful thoughts, fears, and limiting beliefs, the easier changing your life will become. Our thoughts really do create our reality, because they create either positive or negative feelings. Based on these feelings, we then act out in our life accordingly.

Let's take a look at how our behaviors come about. First, there is a circumstance over which we have little, if any, control. Based on the facts of the circumstance, we have either positive or negative thoughts. Our thoughts then create a feeling that is either positive or negative. Based on these feelings, we take action, or behave in a certain way. The problem is that oftentimes, we are completely unaware of the effect our negative thoughts have on our behavior. We might not even be aware that we are thinking these thoughts, because they are so deeply engrained in our subconscious. This is what I call living on autopilot.

Our suffering is not caused by our circumstances; our suffering is caused by our thoughts about our circumstances. Our thoughts are incredibly powerful. Where your thoughts go, so, too, will you.

Though we may not have the power to control someone else, we surely have the power to control our thoughts. But first, we have to become aware of the thoughts that are causing our suffering. We need to recognize where and when our stressful thoughts show up. Are we thinking about someone else and what they should be doing or how they should be behaving? Are our thoughts busy taking care of someone else's life? And when we are over there in their business, who is taking care of usiness? No one. We neglect the things in our own life that need attention.

In the case of your husband's porn addiction, I don't want to discount how his actions have caused your suffering. But that doesn't mean you can't look at how your own thoughts are making that suffering even worse. Examining your own thoughts has nothing to do with making your husband's hurtful actions ok. Remember, his behavior is out of your control. But your thoughts are within your control. It would serve you to see if they are helping you in a positive way, or are they are adding to your suffering. How much mental energy are you spending obsessing about your husband's behavior?

Author and spiritual teacher Byron Katie, who I'll talk more about later, teaches that there are three types of business: his business, your business, and God's business. I will demonstrate the differences using a benign example of neighbors and their lawns. Your neighbor's grass is growing tall and looking unkempt. You think to yourself, "My neighbor should mow his lawn because I am tired of seeing that mess." You're getting stressed out just looking at it.

Now let's break this down. Whose business is it if your neighbor cuts his grass? *His business.* Whose business is it if you get stressed out looking at his unkempt lawn? *Your business.* Whose business is it if the rain falls and the sun shines to make the grass grow fast? *God's business.* You will know when you are in someone else's business because you will feel anxious. You are looking to the other person to do something so that you will feel better. You are trying to control someone else, when, as I've said, the only person you can control is yourself.

Let's talk about your inner judge. She is that really hateful voice in your head that loves to throw insults at you and everyone else. She is your negative script on steroids. Always judging others for this and that, always at the ready to tell everyone else what they "should" or "should not" do; she can be really harsh. As a matter of fact, she is hardest on you. She says things to you that you would never say to anyone else. You have heard her. She has been slinging some serious mud at you your whole life—and especially now, since discovering your husband's porn addiction. She is telling you that his addiction is your fault.

Your inner judge has been filling you with so many lies. And I have a serious hunch that you may believe her. "You caused his addiction." "If you were better in the sack, he wouldn't have started using porn." "You drove him to use porn because you have gained so much weight." "You are fat and ugly." The list of self-deprecating judgments goes on and on. Your relationship with your inner judge goes way back, and she has provided you with a whole playlist of limiting beliefs that you live by. We all have an inner judge. You are not alone in this.

Stressful thoughts, fears, and limiting beliefs have caused me a world of pain. I have believed all the lies, created an inner religion of suffering and limitation, which has led me to make many bad decisions. There are so many dreams I have let pass me by because my limiting beliefs were there to stop me from going after what I wanted. "You aren't capable of making great things happen in your life." "You are just a small town girl who isn't good enough." "You need a man to take care of you."

Because I believed these lies, I held myself back. I settled for less than what I was truly capable of, and I lived small. I followed the voice of my inner judge instead of the voice of my Higher Self far too many times, and it has caused me a whole lot of suffering. To cope with the pain, I used drugs and alcohol to numb myself. I was too afraid to face my fears and prove that voice wrong. At the time, I didn't understand this was happening. I had no idea that I was living on autopilot. It wasn't until I started a path of self-discovery that a light was shone on my self-sabotaging behaviors, and it was then I was able to see myself through the lens of awareness.

Through self-awareness, I was able to own my own crap. I stared fear in the face and moved forward courageously. Finally, I am living my life in alignment with what I truly want. My inner judge has not been silenced, nor has my negative script. They are both still with me, chiming in whenever they can. Those voices haven't changed one bit. But I have changed. Awareness and self-love have changed me. I have learned to control those voices rather than letting them control me. I don't always do life perfectly, but I do my best to remember that happiness is an inside job, and that my freedom depends on me.

I have helped many clients along their own path of self-discovery to find their own freedom through self-awareness. Read on, and I can help you, too. I can be your guide, but you have to be willing to do the heavy lifting. Change is up to you.

If you are ready, we can start with bringing awareness to your thoughts, judgments, and limiting beliefs. The road might be a bit bumpy and you may feel uncomfortable, but you need to be willing to feel discomfort in order to create change in your life. No one changes when they are comfortable. This is how you start to take back your life.

You have a lot going on in your mind. The best thing for you to do is to write it all down. Get it out of your head and onto paper. If you've been keeping a journal, as I suggested earlier, you probably already have plenty of material for filling out these exercises. If not, get started writing now.

These exercises will help you uncover your stressful thoughts and limiting beliefs. When doing these exercises, allow your inner judge to express herself as she usually would. Don't censor this voice. Don't worry about being spiritual, politically correct, or kind. For this purpose, letting your inner judge run wild will actually help you.

Exercise: Read each statement below, and then list the first thoughts/beliefs that pop into your mind. Simplify each thought to one sentence. Shoot for five thoughts/beliefs for each statement—but it's okay if you have more. There are no right or wrong thoughts/beliefs. It is important you do these exercises because you will be working with them in the next chapter.

Example: *My husband is a porn addict. What this means about our marriage:*

1. I will never be able to trust him again.
2. We will never get back to the way we were.
3. Our marriage is a lie.
4. Our children have lost their family.
5. Our marriage is over.

Statement: *My husband is a porn addict. What this means about our marriage:*

1.
2.
3.
4.
5.

Statement: *My husband is a porn addict. What this means about him:*

1.
2.
3.
4.
5.

Statement: *My husband is a porn addict. What this means about me:*

1.
2.
3.
4.
5.

Statement: *My husband is a porn addict. What this means about my future:*

1.
2.
3.
4.
5.

Exercise: Should I Stay or Should I Go Fears List. You may be struggling with either or both of these choices. One way to find clarity is to get the fears out of your head and onto paper. Fill out a list for either or both of the statements. Simplify each fear to one sentence. These fears will come from your negative script so, again, let that voice speak uncensored. In the next chapter you will learn how to tackle these fears.

Statement: *If I stay in my marriage, I fear that these things will happen:*

1.
2.
3.
4.
5.

Statement: *If I leave my marriage, I fear that these things will happen:*

1.
2.
3.
4.
5.

Doing these exercises will prepare you to move on to the next step. It is time to kick your stressful thoughts to the curb.

Go to www.sandybrowncoaching.com/paw-bonus for the free download of these exercises.

CHAPTER 6:

Mindset Reset

"The world as we have created it is a process of our thinking. It cannot be changed without changing our thinking."
Albert Einstein

Suffering is a choice. A difficult truth to accept but all the same, it is the truth. Even in the devastation of your husband's betrayal, you have the power to choose how much you want to suffer. How long will you stay in bed with the covers pulled over your head feeling like a victim? Are you ready to stand up and say, "Screw it! I'm taking my life back!"? You don't have to wait for your husband's recovery before you decide to be ok. He could be jerking off to his porn right now and you can still choose to be ok. Your peace of mind is your responsibility. It isn't going to come from anyone else but you. You have the power to change your life, and it starts with changing your thinking.

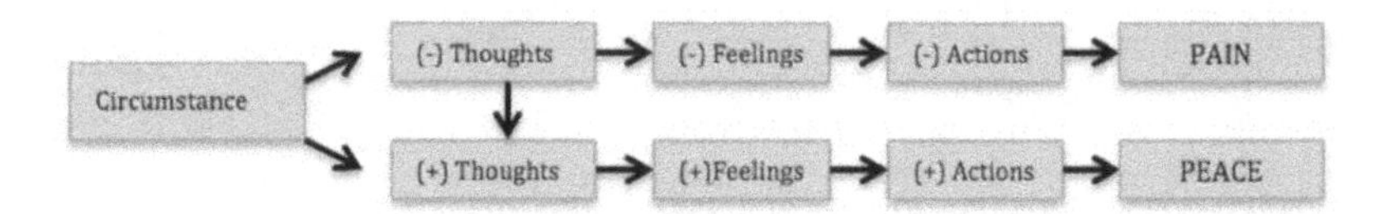

The diagram above is an example of the power of thought. No matter the circumstance, you get to choose either a path of pain or a path of peace, depending on the thoughts you choose. While you have no control over the circumstances, you do have control over your thoughts. When you aren't mindful of your thoughts in any given situation, you are in reaction mode. Your thoughts are choosing for you. That is autopilot thinking. Don't like the results? You can choose again. You can switch that negative thought to a positive thought and create a path to peace.

This isn't a new concept. Albert Einstein understood it, and many gurus and spiritual teachers have been teaching it for eons. There is no way to get around it. If you want to be free of suffering, you have to take responsibility for your thinking. No more blaming it on circumstances or on anyone else. The responsibility is yours alone.

I always hated it when my first husband would say to me, "I'm not responsible for how you feel." It made my blood boil, and I wanted to haul off and smack him. But after learning that my thoughts create my feelings, I had to admit he was right. I have to take responsibility for my own thoughts, even those that drove me to feeling aggravated enough to want to smack him. Learning to change your thoughts isn't going to happen overnight, but you can learn to implement some powerful tools that will get you there. The problem with your negative thoughts (script) is that you will always have them, especially when you are under stress. You can't eliminate negative thoughts, but you can learn to deal with them.

Back in 2002, I was introduced to a book called *Loving What Is*, by Byron Katie. This book outlines an inquiry process developed by Byron Katie that she calls The Work™. This is a simple but powerful process.

Through the systematic questioning of your judgments and stressful thoughts, doing The Work™ will bring you clarity and peace of mind. At first glance, I found it hard to believe. Then, I was facilitated through the process of questioning my own stressful thought. After a short 20-minute process, I felt a remarkable shift in myself! I went from feeling completely stressed out to feeling at peace. I wouldn't have believed it if I hadn't experienced it firsthand. I was so blown away by the experience that I went home and booked my space in the very next School for The Work™, which would be held three months later.

Enrolling in a school like this was not a regular thing for me to do. Prior to this I would never have spent this kind of money on myself. Not to mention, it required me to be away from my young children for nine days. Leaving my kids for this long was a big deal for me, because the longest I had ever been away from my babies was for "one" overnight trip over 11 years. But I was in a really low place in my life, and I was tired of suffering through it. At the time, I was still married to my first husband and we had a toxic marriage. He was emotionally abusive and had substance abuse issues that were not getting any better despite 12-step programs and marriage counseling. After years of waiting for him to change, I was desperate to find a solution that would help me get clear so I could put an end to my suffering.

It was at The School for The Work™ where I truly learned that my suffering was not caused by my circumstances; rather, my suffering was caused by my thoughts about my circumstances. I had a very painful "story" about my marriage. This story was a string of fearful thoughts and limiting beliefs that was keeping me stuck in fear. I was angry with my ex-husband for so many things that he had done both to me and to our relationship.

While at the school, I learned that while he may have done something to me one time, I did it to myself over and over again with every replay in my head. My focus was on his behavior. And I was causing myself all kinds of stress because of it. I'm not saying that his behavior was ok, but my thoughts about his behavior were causing me more pain than the initial event. I had been stuck in my story.

Katie facilitated many brave individuals through her inquiry process. They questioned their stories and I witnessed each person find peace by taking responsibility for his/her part in their suffering. The truth is that our own thinking causes more pain in our lives than anyone else's actions or any situation does. For the first time, I could clearly see my part in my own suffering. I questioned my negative thoughts and limiting beliefs like nobody's business (ha-ha, because I was focused on my own business).

It is important to have awareness of our painful stories. At the time, my story went like this: "I am stuck in this toxic marriage. I can't make it on my own because I have no career, and haven't worked for almost a decade since choosing to be a stay-at-home mom. It wouldn't be fair to my kids to deprive them of their comfortable lifestyle. I am stuck with no way out."

My first painful thought was, "I am stuck in this toxic marriage." With this thought in mind, my negative script found all the proof it needed to make that thought seem true. All those thoughts strung together created my story about being stuck in a toxic marriage. And that was not my only story. I had many painful stories that were creating pain and chaos in my life. There was also the "I'm not good enough" and the "I'm not worthy" stories that I had been telling myself for a lifetime. With these and other stories, I built my own prison and threw away the key. I was paralyzed with fear and couldn't make a decision to save my life.

I had to learn to break myself free from the imprisonment of my own making! Self-inquiry taught me about the pain my thoughts were creating in my life. With this awareness, I was able to identify my painful thoughts and then take them to inquiry. Questioning my thoughts using The Work™ was the key to my freedom. Living on autopilot, I had never noticed how I just accepted my painful thoughts as truth. I just believed them. (Remember, belief has *lie* in the middle of it.) My thoughts were controlling me instead of me controlling my thoughts. Because of them, I was accepting all that unnecessary suffering. All the while I was blaming my ex-husband for my pain and I couldn't see that I was causing much of my own pain.

After doing The Work™, my mind became clearer and I felt stronger. I was no longer held back by my painful story of limitation, and I was able to reach the difficult decisions I needed to make regarding my toxic marriage. This process of inquiry really does clear your mind and, most amazingly, frees you from suffering. It isn't an exaggeration to tell you that the transformation through this process is powerful. You can experience this transformation, too.

You will serve yourself best to approach this process of inquiry with an open heart and an open mind. As an attendee of The School, I am a trained facilitator. I have facilitated many clients through this powerful process and they were able to make remarkable changes in their lives because of it. My clients learned that suffering truly is a choice and with this knowledge they were empowered to take control of their lives.

The self-inquiry process of The Work™ is very simple, with just four questions and some turnarounds:

1. Is it true?
2. Can you absolutely know that it's true?
3. How do you react when you believe that thought?
4. Who would you be without the thought?

And then:

Turn it around.

Question number three is my favorite. When you really dig deep into it, you can analyze your behaviors caused by believing the negative thought. While working on question three, ask yourself questions like:

1. What does this belief feel like in your body? Where do you feel it?
2. How are you treating other people and even yourself when you believe this thought?
3. How do you act out because of this thought?
4. Where is this thought holding you back?

Dig deep and ask yourself these and other probing questions. As you dig, pay attention to other limiting beliefs that you uncover and write them down. You can question those beliefs later. Believe me, you will unearth many long-held, limiting beliefs as you work question number three.

After you have excavated all you can in regard to your behaviors from believing the thought, move on to question number four. This is where you get to use your imagination to see other ways of being while in the same circumstances. Ask yourself the same questions as above, but from the perspective of being *without* the painful thought. Allow yourself to see how you might behave differently if you couldn't even think that thought. You will most likely discover a more peaceful and happier version of yourself. You may see that you do have a choice!

Now that you have experienced a little freedom from the painful thought with question four, now you get to play with what Katie calls the turnarounds. You turn the original thought to the opposite, other, and self. Then, with each revised thought, you look for proof or examples of how this new thought might be just as true or truer than your original thought.

In case you are confused, I will demonstrate how to do The Work™ with one of my own painful thoughts about my husband, Ted. My painful thought is: "*My husband should pay more attention to me.*" First, I ask myself, "*Is it true?*" While it feels true to me, when I look beyond the surface of the thought, I can see that I can't say for certain that I would be better off if my husband paid more attention to me. So my answer is, "No," this thought is not absolutely true.

Next, I ask myself, *"Sandy, how do you react when you believe this thought?"* I take myself to a moment in time when I really believe this thought. My answer: I notice my heart closes off and my chest feels tight. My shoulders tense and I clinch my jaw. When my husband is around, I am cold and distant. I give him short answers and treat him like the enemy. I say mean things about him in my mind like, "He is such an idiot," "Maybe if he pulled his head out of his ass he might actually notice me." (See how I let the inner judge run wild?) Then I start saying mean things about myself like, "If I was ten pounds lighter... ," or "Who would pay attention to a fatty like you?" When I believe this thought I am short with the kids, I blow little things out of proportion, and I slam the cupboard doors. I refuse to do nice things for my husband. I leave the room and ignore him. Instead of talking to him about how I'm feeling, I shut him out and then I blame him for it.

Next, I ask myself, *"Sandy, who would you be without that thought?"* My answer: I would be lighter and more playful. I would be more welcoming to my husband when he walked in the room. I would be helpful and loving. I would deal with things as they came up, and I would thoughtfully respond without blowing up. I would be more peaceful and patient. I think I would be more fun to be around! My heart is open, my shoulders loose, and my jaw is no longer clenched. I feel so much better without the thought.

Now that I am feeling more peaceful, it is time to do the turnarounds of my original thought.

- ✓ Turnaround to the opposite: *My husband should pay more attention to me* turns into *My husband shouldn't pay more attention to me.* Who wants to pay attention to that mean-spirited, withdrawn, explosive version of me? I wouldn't want to spend time with someone behaving like that. I wouldn't want to pay attention to anyone who was acting like that. I am just fine whether my husband pays attention to me or not. It is only when I think he "should" be different than he is that I start to feel rattled

- ✓ Turn around to the other. *My husband should pay more attention to me* turns into *I should pay more attention to my husband.* Yes, there are plenty of times when he tries to get me to spend more time with him, but I am too busy with the kids or my work. He works really hard, and I don't show him often enough how much I appreciate all he does. Often, at the end of the day, I get lost in TV shows instead of having a conversation with my husband.
- ✓ Turnaround to self. *My husband should pay more attention to me* turns into *I should pay more attention to myself.* When was the last time I went to the doctor for a regular check-up? Or the dentist, for that matter? I often say yes to other people when I really want to say no. I take on more than I can handle because I want to please others. I can't remember the last time I did something just because it brought me joy. I need to pay more attention to myself because that is my job.

Did you notice the shift in my thinking? While my original painful thought was all about judging my husband, the turnarounds brought the thought back to me. It is my job to pay attention to myself and to find my own peace of mind. Not anyone else's.

If you want to learn more about Byron Katie, pick up a copy of her book, *Loving What Is.* The book is loaded with examples of Katie facilitating people through The Work™. My favorite version is the audio book. Hearing Katie facilitate the work is far more beneficial than reading it alone, because you can actually hear the transformation and you will better understand the process. Also, you can visit www.thework.com to find more information on The Work™.

Once you have a solid understanding for doing The Work™, you can use it to question your thoughts and fears from the exercises you completed in chapter five. Doing The Work™ on your thoughts about your husband will help you get clear and will help you make decisions you need to make regarding the future of your relationship. But, before you work on those very important thoughts, it is good to practice on other thoughts that don't hold so much weight.

A great place to start for beginners is in looking at your judgments of situations and other people. Your inner judge will provide plenty of material there. How many times a day do you find yourself giving others advice on how they could live better, even if only in your mind? Judgments of others work great because you can be assured that in the turnarounds, it will be brought back to you—because it is you that you need to work on.

If you are going to take your judgments to inquiry, give yourself permission to judge others and your husband with reckless abandon. Don't worry about being politically correct or spiritual. Let your inner judge go wild. You can learn a great deal about yourself from your judgments, because your judgments are often projections of what you neglect or reject in yourself.

Start paying attention to all your thoughts. Question the *should/shouldn't*, *have to*, *can/can't*, *always/never* and *need them to* thoughts. The possibilities are endless. One word of caution: hold off on self-judgments until you have a full understanding of The Work™ or until an experienced facilitator can walk you through it. Self-judgments are tricky to work with and need to be handled with care if you are to receive the most healing from them.

Self-inquiry is not just a situational tool to use when you are in crisis mode. You will serve yourself best by developing the habit of questioning your painful thoughts. Some people treat inquiry as a form of meditation and they do it every day. This could become your spiritual practice.

Get in the practice of being very mindful of your thoughts. Remember to become the self-observer. When you start to notice you believe your painful story, step back and tell yourself, "There is that stressful story again." Dissect all the thoughts that are a part of that story and give the entire story a name. "That is my *not good enough* story, or my *I need him to be different if I'm going to be happy* story." Learn to be very present in the moment and take control of your thoughts.

Be the change you want to see. Don't wait for your husband to change. Take charge of your life! Do you want to be happy? Then change your thinking. Remember that you get to choose which path you take, peace or pain. It all begins with your thoughts. Quit blaming your husband for all your suffering. Take responsibility for your own pain and get to work. The only reason you are stuck in fear is because you are making the choice to be stuck in fear. Question your thoughts and you will find the answers you need. You will break free from your self-imposed prison and you will be able to make the big decisions you need to make. Through self- inquiry you can make those decisions from a place of strength. Take your power back! Take your life back!

Once you have a solid understanding of The Work™, I want you to use it on your painful thoughts and fears from your completed chapter 5 exercises. With a better understanding of yourself, you will find a better understanding of your husband. With this new understanding, you may be ready to start thinking about forgiving him.

CHAPTER 7:

Forgiveness - Moving from Fear to Love

"I will never forgive that bastard!" Sound familiar? I thought this, too—and so have many of my clients. If you are still raw from your husband's betrayal, forgiving him may be the farthest thing from your mind. It may seem unimaginable to ever reach a state of mind where you could ever forgive him. The fact is that forgiveness will never come from your mind, because that is where your fear lives. In order to forgive, it has to come from your heart where Love (as in God is Love) lives.

There is a sense of power in withholding forgiveness. You may think that if you forgive him, you will be sending a message that what your husband did is ok. Your mind wants you to believe that by casting him out of your heart, you are protecting yourself from further harm. You want him to suffer the way you are suffering right now. To forgive your husband would make it too easy on him. You want him to feel your pain; you want him to know what it feels like to be betrayed and victimized. His actions have left you feeling vulnerable and helpless. It feels safe to hold on to this false sense of power that comes from your anger, your blame, and your self-righteousness.

Would you believe me if I told you that withholding forgiveness is hurting you more than it is helping you? The truth is, your unwillingness to forgive keeps you stuck in the pain of his betrayal. You are choosing to relive the experience over and over again. You replay his betrayal again and again in your mind. Yes, he did it to you, but you do it to yourself every time you run the replay in your mind. Your unwillingness to forgive is your jailor, and you will never be free until you forgive him.

Withholding forgiveness is like drinking poison and expecting the other person to die. You will have no peace without forgiveness. Because you are holding on to your pain, you are unable to truly move forward with your life. These are some difficult things to point out, but I would not be serving you to the best of my ability if I don't at least open you up to these truths. You don't have to buy into this 100%. Just think about the possibility that you may be choosing to remain a victim through withholding forgiveness for your husband. There is no power in victimhood.

It didn't do me any good to remain a victim to my husband's betrayal. Through my own recovery work, I had to give myself a kick in the ass by facing the reality that I am nobody's victim. I expect my clients to do the same. If I am to be a great coach, I have to be brave enough to tell my clients what they *need* to hear not what they *want* to hear. They may not like it at first, but eventually, they learn that I am telling them the truth. I will not do any less for you. Like I said, where you are right now in discovery, you may not want to think about forgiveness. Just take a bite for now and you can always come back for more when you are ready. Stay with me if only to see the possibilities.

Joy and happiness can be yours once again, but not when you are stuck in your pain. The good news is that it doesn't have to be this way. You can forgive your husband and still hold him accountable. If you are going to stick it out and work through this together, your forgiveness will serve you both. You can forgive him and still choose that you do not want to stay in your marriage. The way to take your life back is through forgiveness. This is how you reclaim your real power, because it takes courage and strength to forgive. The choice is, of course, yours, but holding onto the belief that forgiveness is a sign of weakness is hurting you. I invite you to let it go.

"Do you want to be right or do you want to be happy?"
Marianne Williamson

This is one of my favorite teachings: forgiveness is the most loving thing you can do for yourself. Happiness comes from forgiveness. When you withhold forgiveness, you are blocking your happiness. Some might say that forgiveness is a selfish act. I'm going to tell you that this is a good kind of selfish. Don't forgive him because you want to be self-righteous by being the better person. Forgive him because you want to feel better.

If that isn't enough to convince you to forgive your husband, I ask you, "What would Jesus do?" Yes, I pulled the Jesus card. Not because I want to throw any kind of religious dogma at you–that is not what I am about. But because, regardless of your religious beliefs, I think we both can agree that Jesus was a walking, talking, forgiving machine. He was the expression of unconditional Love here on this earth. You don't have to believe in Jesus to see the value in his teachings about forgiveness.

I mentioned earlier in the book that my spiritual practice is the study of *A Course in Miracles,* which is not only a psychological retraining of the brain but a spiritual teaching that embraces the universal truths of all religions. While its main references are to Christianity through Christ and the Holy Spirit, I see it more as a teaching of Christ Consciousness. Whether you believe in Jesus Christ as the savior or not, I think it is possible to see him as a great teacher of Love. His teachings are lessons that cross all religious barriers and are there for us to find our way to true joy and happiness through Love. Marianne Williamson is Jewish and she is one of the most prominent teachers of *A Course in Miracles.*

You cannot get what you are not giving. The world we live in has taught us that to give means we are losing something. But to believe this is to believe a lie. I don't think it is any accident that forgiveness has the word "give" in the middle of it. When you give something to someone else, it grows in you. You literally have to give "it" away–be it love, joy or forgiveness–in order for it to grow in you. That is why it is so much better to give than to receive. This is demonstrated in your unwillingness to forgive your husband. You are afraid that you will lose your sense of security if you forgive him; but what you withhold from him, you withhold from yourself. Withholding forgiveness creates a prison for both him and you. There is no security in that.

Your husband may not deserve your forgiveness for all the pain he has caused. But, when you can forgive your husband for his betrayal, forgiveness will grow in you. For what actions of your own have you not forgiven yourself? We all have these skeletons in our closet. I know there is something from your past you are probably beating yourself up about. You haven't been able to forgive yourself, have you? Can you see the correlation between forgiving others and forgiving yourself?

Let this be your opportunity to forgive yourself by extending the gift of forgiveness to your husband. Allow your forgiveness for him to heal you. The beauty is that whether he does anything with your forgiveness or not, the love and forgiveness you extended to him will expand in you. Are you willing to allow yourself to be selfish enough to forgive your husband? Has the door to forgiveness cracked open just a little bit?

When have you needed forgiveness from someone else? I can remember a time when something I did hurt my husband deeply. I didn't even do it to him directly, but my actions had a very hurtful effect on him. It was one of my mindless tequila moments. No, I didn't cheat on him. But, I felt terrible for hurting him and, because he was hurting, I was trapped in pain. When he finally saw past his own pain to forgive me, I felt free to forgive myself.

I'll say it again: the only way to have joy and happiness is through forgiveness. You extend forgiveness to heal your life. The bonus is that by extending it, you offer your husband the opportunity to heal as well. You offer him the opportunity to break free from his own prison created by his addiction. Whether he decides to forgive himself is not your business. Your only function is to forgive. Forgiveness allows you to move forward with a clear mind and an open-heart, no longer blocking Love from your experience. Forgive your husband because it is the right thing to do for you.

If you still aren't ready to forgive your husband, let's try to loosen the death grip fear has on your heart. I know you don't give a flying fig that your husband may be feeling pain because of his addiction. You want him to feel pain. I get it. But remember, as long as you are wishing him harm you are harming yourself too. Eventually, there will come a point when you want to be free from your pain and suffering.

Let's talk in general terms. Can we agree that most every adult has childhood wounds that have not yet been healed? I am willing to guess you have these wounds as well. And so does your husband. Your wounds may be around the belief that you aren't good enough, worthy enough, loveable enough, smart enough, pretty enough... the list goes on. Even as adults, we want to find relief from the wounds of our childhood. We have never been taught how to heal these wounds, so they fester just below the surface until something bumps that small protective layer. Then, the wound is once again raw and open. Sometimes it only takes that negative script in your own head to open those wounds, almost as though that script loves nothing more than to cause you pain by stabbing and jabbing those wounds. You might be sailing along in life without a care in the world until something happens to open that old wound, and all those old painful feelings come rushing to the surface.

We think we are in pain because of our current circumstances. In reality, that old pain we have been holding onto for years, if not decades, has been *triggered* by our current circumstances. The pain carries such a punch that we want to get away from it at any cost.

I know I felt that way. I was a weed addict for many a year before I decided to deal with my pain in a healthy way. I actually did quite a bit of work with my old wounds, but not enough–because some years later after quitting my weed addiction, I became a wine junkie. Emotional pain is like an onion, you can peel layer upon layer away but if you stop, you won't get to the core of the problem. After peeling back a few layers you may feel better, but if you don't keep peeling, sooner or later the pain will start to feel more intense and you will feel the need to either fight it or flee it. Many of us flee the pain by finding a substance to numb it. Any substance will do, be it drugs, shopping, gambling, drama, food, porn, or work.

If you could see even the slightest possibility that your husband could be suffering from his own unhealed, childhood wounds, would you be able to forgive him? What if, just like you or anyone else, he has his own story of not being enough? Could you see that he may be feeling just as desperate as anyone else to numb the pain so he can feel better about himself?

Your husband may not show his insecurities on the outside, because he is trying to live up to the macho expectation that a man is never to show his vulnerability; however, is it possible that the inner child in him could be in unbearable pain? In chapter 2, you learned that porn is a drug and that habitual use is an addiction. Dr. Gabor Mate` states that all addiction is caused because the user is running from pain, as he explains beautifully in a YouTube video called *What Is Addiction? (Gabor Mate`).*

Let's look at forgiveness from another perspective. An attack is a cry for love. Addiction is actually an attack on oneself. Yes, we think it is helping us, but it is really harming us in ways we cannot even imagine. Our pain is a cry for love. All we want in life is to feel loved and to be happy. But for many of us, our negative script tells us we are not worthy of love or of happiness because we are not enough.

In general terms, I think that when you can relate to the pain of childhood wounds and can see that most everyone suffers from unhealed, childhood trauma, you may begin to have compassion for addicts in general. You are a kind and loving person. I know you can find even just a sliver of compassion for those you see who have fallen in the trap of addiction as a way of escaping their pain. Can you see their behavior as a cry for love? There is a part of them that hates themselves, and they have to run from that pain. No matter how much someone else may love them, it is never enough if they do not love themselves.

For some, this can be an unbearable pain. These people can quickly fall under the spell of any drug let alone a powerful drug such as internet porn. It is available, affordable, and anonymous. For most people, they can use internet porn and get back to their day without anyone being the wiser. Pain relief comes with just one quick click. It doesn't get any easier to use a drug than that.

Now, can you allow yourself to see that your husband may be one of those people I just described? Even if for just a minute, can you see there may be some truth to what I am saying? Could you possibly see that your husband is good at his core, even though his brain has been hijacked? Could you possibly show your husband the same compassion you would show any drug addict? I'm not saying you have to, I am only asking you to open yourself to the possibility. You may not be ready yet. But when you are, how will you know?

You will know you are ready to forgive your husband:

- ✓ When you finally realize the pain you are holding onto is hurting you more than it is hurting your husband.
- ✓ When you are finally ready to let go of your suffering.
- ✓ When you accept the past is in the past and you realize it does not serve you to dwell in the past.
- ✓ When you make the decision to step out of fear and into Love.
- ✓ When you realize that the only way out of your pain is through forgiveness.

Forgiveness starts with your willingness to see your husband another way. When you can do this, miracles will start to happen. You will have chosen to create something new for yourself and for your own healing.

Many of my clients have found that they don't even have to be 100% sure they are ready to forgive. They have learned to take the first step in the direction of forgiveness through their willingness to end their own suffering. They make the decision that it is more important to heal than to make their husband suffer and they realize their need for attacking him is no longer serving them. By this point, my clients have done enough of their mindset work that they are prepared to fearlessly move forward with their lives. With this new perception they are willing to step out of fear and into Love.

When my clients have decided they are ready to move closer to forgiveness, there are two techniques I like to teach them, which I will share with you. First, it is important that you know forgiveness isn't a single act. Forgiveness is a process. Even if you start off with a half-hearted effort, each day you practice these techniques you will forgive a little more until you have reached true forgiveness, when you completely let go of the offense and you are truly free from its effects.

The first technique I learned from Marianne Williamson. Pray for your husband's happiness every day.

(Sound effect of needle scratching record.) Say whaaaat?

Yes, pray for your husband's happiness every day for 30 days. At the end of those 30 days, I cannot guarantee that your husband will have changed one tiny bit. But I am willing to bet that something in you *has* changed. There is a reason Jesus said, "Pray for your enemies." It is how you heal yourself. Add to this prayer a commitment not to speak ill of your husband to others or even in your mind. Stick with this undertaking as best you can. Progress not perfection. One day at a time. If you screw up and say something bad about him, you get to start over in the very next moment. Remember that every moment of every day brings you an opportunity to begin again. Keep praying every day even if you slip up. Don't let a little mistake stop you from making great progress. Catch yourself, forgive yourself, and move on.

Your prayer might sound like this:

Dear Higher Power,
I pray for ______'s happiness that he should receive everything he needs to feel whole and blessed. May every blessing be bestowed upon him for his highest and best good. And so it is. Amen

The second technique is an ancient Hawaiian practice called Ho'Oponopono. It is a type of prayer as well. The foundation of Ho'Oponopono is to take 100% responsibility for your life. That means that you have to take total responsibility for attracting everything–every situation and every person–into your life, whether they caused pain or not.

(Very LOUD sound effect of record scratching.) No fricking way!

You might be thinking, "I did not ask my husband to cause me this pain." Don't get your knickers in a twist, because your thinking is correct. You are not responsible for your husband using internet porn, then becoming a porn addict, which resulted in his betrayal that caused you so much pain. Let's reframe this.

Earlier I stated that when we judge others, we are projecting onto them something that we are rejecting in ourselves. What we see in front of us is a mirror reflecting back to us what we are neglecting to heal in ourselves. We all have old programs that are with us on an unconscious level. (We might call them our old wounds.) When you notice something in your husband that you don't like, you can bet that you have that in yourself. You both share that program on an unconscious level. As soon as you start to feel irritated with your husband—or anyone else for that matter—that is your cue to say the Ho'Oponopono prayer. Practicing Ho'Oponopono is an exercise in cleaning up your life, which is the only way to become a whole person. When you do the prayer, you are cleaning the program in yourself and that healing energy is also cleaning up the program in your husband. Your forgiveness is his forgiveness! The prayer is very simple.

I Love you. I'm sorry. Please forgive me. Thank you

You say the prayer in silence, and you are saying it to the Divine (Higher Power). You are not saying it to your husband. You have noticed something in your husband that is irritating the crap out of you. Knowing the program you see in him is what you need to clear in yourself, you call upon the Divine by saying, "I love you." Then you say, "I'm sorry." You are apologizing to the Divine because until now, you were not conscious of this program in you that needed to be cleared. "Forgive me" for not being aware. You then say, "thank you," because gratitude is powerful and magnifies your healing. Accepting responsibility for everything in your life is the hard part. Saying the prayer is very easy.

If you find the power of this practice to be a bit hard to believe, look up the story of Dr. Hew Len. He healed an entire psych ward for the criminally insane by using nothing but the practice of Ho'Oponopono. It is a miraculous story.

I would like to talk more about attracting relationships into our lives. Another way to look at your relationship with your husband is to realize that relationships are assignments from the Universe bringing you lessons for your soul's growth. On an unconscious level, we attract what we need in our life. This is why I suggest it is important to heal your childhood wounds through this relationship with your husband because if you don't, you will probably attract someone else who may look different on the outside, but on the inside he is bringing you the same gifts.

If you want to truly heal your old wounds you have to take 100% responsibility for your life, do your work, and learn your lessons. Sure, you can run–but you are only putting off the inevitable. That lesson will show up another day brought to you by another person. Why not just get it over with now?

Of course, the exception to this is if you're in a physically abusive relationship. I would never suggest anyone stay in a relationship such as that. In this case, leave and do your work from afar–but don't jump into another relationship until you have healed.

If you still aren't ready to forgive your husband, be aware that you are still living in and holding on to fear. You are living your life from that negative script in your head. Your Higher Power is a blazing light within you, and is only a heartbeat away. Your Higher Self is connected to this light, and it knows that forgiveness is the only way to happiness. When you are in pain, it can be difficult to step out of your mind and into your heart because your negative script will tell you, "No, don't do it. You are not safe." But once you connect to that light within, you will know that living from Love will provide you all the safety you need.

You can use your Inner Guidance Meter to test whether you are ready to forgive your husband or not. See what your body has to say. Remember that your body will never lie to you. It always knows your truth.

Envision yourself sometime in the future when you have forgiven your husband. Let this scenario fill every cell in your body and experience it with all of your senses. Drop into your body to see *what* you are feeling and *where* you are feeling it. Then give it a number on the scale from -10 to +10. If this number is in the (-) range, it just means you aren't quite ready to forgive. Test yourself on another day and when you find your number is in the (+) range, this is an indicator that you are truly ready to start the forgiveness process.

You don't have to be *ready* to forgive before starting either of the above forgiveness practices. You can start anytime. Practicing them may be exactly what you need to move yourself closer to forgiveness. There is no set timeframe for when you should be ready to forgive your husband. The only question to ask yourself is, "Am I willing to let go of this pain?" I suppose you could decide to never forgive your husband. If that is your choice, be willing to take responsibility for choosing to stay stuck in the pain of his betrayal.

If your husband is working on himself and really making an effort, your unwillingness to forgive will be holding you both in a prison of suffering. If he is making every effort to repair your relationship and you want that too, take that leap of faith and trust this process enough to forgive him. Regardless of his efforts, your forgiveness will bring you clarity, happiness, and freedom to move forward.

Do you want to be right or happy?

My husband has told me that my acceptance and forgiveness of him gave him hope that we had a chance to rebuild our relationship. He wanted our relationship to heal. Because of my forgiveness, he found the courage to face the pain he caused and was able to fight his addiction. But that isn't why I forgave him. I forgave him for myself. I wanted to be free of my suffering. I was working my own program and because of it, I chose happiness over being right.

If you are both working your own recovery, you will find that you are both showing up in your relationship as better versions of yourselves. You will be learning to open up and to be more vulnerable with each other. Having done your own work, you will be ready to join your husband in a new way of relating.

CHAPTER 8:

Joining Your Husband in a New Way of Relating

Please keep in mind that while you may be reading this book in the midst of your painful discovery, this chapter is a glimpse into your future should you and your husband decide to work things out. When you both commit to your own respective recoveries, you will be relating to each other in a new way. For now, know that I don't expect you to apply the lessons in this chapter to your life as it is right now. The information in this chapter is intended for use further down your recovery path. However, if you are so moved to apply these lessons right now, it could be very helpful in all areas of your life–especially in difficult conversations with your husband.

The key to creating strong relationships is clear communication. Many relationship problems can be avoided through open, honest, thoughtful communication. If you and your husband are like most couples, your communication skills have been lacking.

In reality, we are never taught how to effectively communicate our needs or our feelings. From an early age, most of us have been modeled dysfunctional communication patterns, which we then adopted without question into our own life. We don't give much thought to how we communicate with our spouse. We just do it, without ever realizing that most of our problems occur because our communication style is dysfunctional.

Clear communication takes effort. Consider your level of awareness of your communication ruts. Have you ever noticed yourself saying, "I don't know why he doesn't get it," yet you probably keep trying to communicate your point the same way every time? The definition of insanity is doing the same thing over and over again, yet expecting different results. It's time to try something different. Having been in recovery, this is the perfect time to develop new communication skills that will actually bring you and your husband closer together. These are great skills to use in all relationships as well.

Clear communication starts with you. Your focus needs to be on developing some basic skills in how you perceive situations, because it is those perceptions that will determine how you communicate. I have found that by following a simple code of conduct in all my interactions, I can avoid unnecessary conflict and save myself a world of hurt. I have incorporated *The Four Agreements* into my life as written by author and spiritual teacher Don Miguel Ruiz. The Four Agreements are:

- ✓ First Agreement: *Be Impeccable with Your Word*
- ✓ Second Agreement: *Don't Take Anything Personally*

- ✓ Third Agreement: *Don't Make Assumptions*
- ✓ Forth Agreement: *Always Do Your Best*

Be Impeccable with Your Word. Your word has immense power. You can think of your word as a double-edged sword. With your word, you can create the most beautiful dream—or you can create a nightmare. If you speak negatively to your husband, you will create war with him. You have attacked him, and now he may feel the need to counterattack. You are now separate forces fighting against each other. On the other hand, if you speak positively to your husband, he will respond to you in kind, and this will bring the two of you together.

Be mindful of what you are saying *about* your husband to other people. Are you using your words to speak positively about him or are you spreading emotional poison by speaking negatively about him to others? You know how it is when you are complaining about your husband to a friend? You get your friend all riled up and angry with your husband. Then the next time your friend sees your husband, she has a negative experience of him because of what you said. You may have forgiven him by then, but she is still mad at him because of the emotional poison you tainted her with.

Be mindful of how you talk to yourself. Are you building yourself up with positive words, or are you tearing yourself down with negative words? You and I both know that we can tear our self-esteem to shreds through our own negative self-talk. This likely never more apparent than at the time of discovering your husband's porn addiction. Yes, you may have blamed him at first and shredded him to ribbons with your words, but afterword, I'm guessing you turned the sword on yourself. There is no greater pain than that caused by our own negative self-talk.

Don't Take Anything Personally. Nothing your husband does is about you—and that includes his porn addiction. Nothing anyone does or even says about you has anything to do with you. Everything is about them. They are acting from their own experience of the world and from their own beliefs and thoughts. Even when they say something good about you or treat you kindly, it isn't about you. If you don't take another person's actions personally, you can avoid the need to defend yourself or the need to create conflict. Just as they are behaving from their own experience, you perceive their actions based on your own past experiences. What they say or do is not necessarily hurting you, but it might feel like it is because it is triggering your old wounds–and that is what you are reacting to. You can avoid a lot of suffering if you don't take things personally.

Here is an example of how I took my husband's actions personally when I shouldn't have. My husband has a thing about a clean kitchen. When he comes home from work, he doesn't like to see dirty dishes in the sink or on the counters. If the sink is full, he starts to complain about it. When he does this, I get defensive and then I attack him. He hasn't said anything about me; he is just upset about the dishes. I take it personally, because the situation has triggered an old wound in me about not being good enough. When I was a kid, my mom wasn't the greatest housekeeper, and I never wanted to have friends over because my house was always a mess and that made me feel less-than. Because of these old wounds, I go to war with my husband over the dishes.

Don't take your husband's porn addiction personally, either. His addiction is not about you. It is important that you remember he is using a drug to run from his problems. Instead of dealing with his pain, he uses porn to numb himself. In that moment, his priority is to feel better. Now, I have a good idea you might be thinking, "But why did he start using in the first place?" I can't give you an exact answer to that, but I can say with a great deal of certainty that it didn't have anything to do with you.

Don't Make Assumptions. We have a tendency to only hear what we want to hear or to see what we want to see based on our past experiences. When our husband says or does something that offends us, we don't bother to ask for clarification because we think we already know his answer. But how could we know? Are we mind readers? I know I am guilty of this. Because I think *I know,* I concoct all kinds of evidence in defense of my assumption. I want to be right at the expense of making him wrong. Before you know it, I have caused an unnecessary rift between us and we aren't talking to each other. I could have avoided this if I had just asked him what his intentions were instead of thinking I already knew his answer. I could have asked him something like this, "When I hear you say ____, I feel________. Is this what you intended?" When you find yourself upset by something your husband has said or done, ask him about it. Give him the opportunity to explain himself. Don't assume you know what your husband is thinking or feeling. Taking that a step further, don't assume you know why he is using porn. Ask him thoughtful questions. You might be surprised by his answers.

Always do your best. Your best will vary from day to day or even minute by minute, especially now that you are in recovery. Accept yourself where you are in every moment. You are learning new ways of relating to your husband, and there will be times when you fall back into dysfunctional patterns, especially when you are under stress. When you catch yourself, you can self-correct. If you realize your error after you have caused a rift with your husband, you can take responsibility for your part and make amends. If you can accept that you are doing your best, you might be able to see that your husband is doing his best as well. I have said it before, and I will say it again: recovery is a process that requires progress, not perfection. Your problems didn't appear overnight and neither will your recoveries. You can only do your best.

Even the best marriages experience conflict. Relationships require two people. Each person comes to the relationship with baggage and with his/her own ideas of how things should be. This is going to cause arguments from time to time. Some arguments will be small, and others may feel like WWIII. The way you argue will determine how much damage those arguments do to your relationship.

We each have our own argument style, which is influenced by our individual temperament. Some people are more passive and others are more aggressive. What I see in my practice is that even when both partners have an aggressive temperament, one will be more so than the other. The important thing to remember is that no matter your temperament, the *way* you argue is what causes the most damage. Common to most dysfunctional communication styles are four relationship killers. If you learn to avoid these, you will save you and your husband a whole lot of unnecessary pain. Remember, if you are reading this in the midst of discovery, you have probably experienced every one of these relationship killers in the last day or so. Understandably, it would be a lot to ask of you to stop using these in heat of this red-hot mess. For now just take them in and keep them in mind for later use.

The first relationship killer is *criticism*. You don't have to attack your partner's personality or character to make your point. In the case of your husband's porn addiction, yes, at first, you're likely to criticize the hell out of him. He is wrong for hurting your relationship this way, and your feelings are understandable. But, for future reference, when you are ready to develop healthier communication, you will want to avoid criticism.

Criticism is about making him wrong and you right. You want to blame him for the way you are feeling. I touched on this in the last chapter. Criticism also shows up through generalizing: "You always _____," or "You never _____" statements. Another way to criticize your husband is to attack him with "You are a (bleep)" statements. When using criticism, a conversation will quickly turn toxic because the other person will feel like they are being attacked and when this happens they go into defensive mode. At this point your partner is not hearing a word you are saying, because they are now busy coming up with their counter-attack. To avoid this attack/counter-attack cycle, learn to complain without blaming. Use

"I" statements and put your focus on relaying what you are feeling and needing from your partner.

The second relationship killer is *contempt*. This is another form of attack. Through contempt, you deem yourself superior by making your partner feel "less than." (Again, in the midst of discovery, you may be feeling nothing but contempt for your husband, and understandably so.) This is accomplished through name-calling, sarcasm, mockery, or hostile humor. Contempt can be shown through your body language, your tone of voice, and eye rolling. Nothing says, "you are a frickin' idiot" like an eye roll. When you fight by using contempt, you may cause damage that is difficult to repair. So try not to do it. Don't set yourself up as superior to your husband, because no one wins when you make him feel like a lower than dirt.

The third relationship killer is *defensiveness*. In order to defend yourself when you perceive you are being attacked, you might throw back your own version of nasty criticism and contemptuous behavior. It is really hard to resist the need to say, "This isn't my fault, it's your fault." Try not to get defensive, otherwise you will find yourself in the cycle of attack/defend/counter-attack and no one wins. Nothing gets accomplished except hurt feelings. Even though you might perceive yourself as being attacked, try to listen to what your partner is saying. Whatever you do, don't react with attack.

The fourth relationship killer is *stonewalling*. This is when one partner, most often the husband, withdraws from the conversation. Have you ever found yourself saying to your partner, "I might as well be talking to a brick wall"? If so, you have probably been stonewalled. Your stonewalling husband will come across as not paying attention or completely tuned out. He has no reaction. Or, he may just walk out of the room. Stonewalling makes the complainer get more aggressive because, "Darn it, you are going to hear me even if I have to chase you down." I know I have been there with my husband. Nothing pisses me off more than being stonewalled. I teach my clients that the best thing to do at this point is to take a time out and regroup. Stonewalling is a sign that your husband is overwhelmed. Men often say that they stonewall because "it is better to say nothing then to say something that will make the situation worse."

If you and your husband have been in the habit of using any or all of these relationship killers, you have felt the damage they cause. But it doesn't have to be that way. I recommend my clients use what I call *Compassionate Communication.* While it may seem easier said than done, it is worth practicing, because when you relate to each other in a more compassionate way, you will make your marriage stronger. After you have both been working your own programs, Compassionate Communication will be easier to put into practice.

With Compassionate Communication, you can avoid judgment and blame. When you need to complain to your husband, don't attack him. Instead, focus on your "I" messages, explain the circumstances as you see it, take responsibility for your own feelings and tell him what you need. "I notice when this happens... I feel... and what I need you to do is ____." There is no attack in the "I" message. There is no bad guy nor is there a victim in Compassionate Communication. There is just you and your husband working together to solve a problem. When it gets down to it, all your husband really wants to know is what the problem is and how he can fix it. Guys are that simple. He just wants to make you happy without being made to feel like a blockhead for having messed up.

Compassionate communication requires you to respond rather than react. When you feel attacked by your husband, resist the urge to counter-attack. I have learned that behind every attack is a cry for love. People attack when they are in a state of fear. So look past the attack to see the fear and you will be able to respond with compassion. If you have been working your program, this is easier to do because you learned that we are rarely upset by our current circumstances. In reality, the circumstances have merely triggered an old, unhealed wound. It will serve both you and your husband to respond to his attack with a compassionate response. Your response might sound like, "What are you really upset about and what do you need?" Your compassionate response will help to diffuse the argument, and you can help your husband get to the root of the problem. This will give him the opportunity to look below the surface and discover what his pain is really about.

Now let's look at how you can use Compassionate Communication when you want to attack your husband for something he did to upset you. As soon as you notice that urge to attack him but before you act on that urge, I want you to "Stop. Drop. And Roll." Stop what you are doing. Drop into your body just as you would when using your Inner Guidance Meter, which you learned in chapter 4. Notice the physical sensations in your body and where you are feeling them. Acknowledge your feelings and ask yourself, "Am I truly upset about _____, or are these old wounds that I am feeling?" "What fears are coming up for me?" Roll with those feelings until you have a better understanding of what you are truly upset about. Stop, Drop and Roll is the most compassionate thing you can do for yourself in that moment.

Realize that your current circumstances are nothing more than a wake-up call for you to go deeper and heal an old wound. That old wound might be related to your fear of not being enough or maybe the fear that you can't depend on anyone. Whatever it is, this is your opportunity to truly heal. The time to approach your husband is when you understand where your pain is coming from. Rather than approaching him in attack mode, you can approach him with Compassionate Communication. Again, using your "I" messages, explain the circumstances as you see them, take responsibility for your own feelings and tell him what you need. "I am noticing that this situation brought up my old wound of ______ and I need you to ______ in order for me to heal. Will you help me?" Now you are working together to heal and solve the problem.

Can you see how Compassionate Communication opens the door to partnership? There is neither a bad guy nor a victim when useing Compassionate Communication. When, instead of blaming the other person, each person takes 100% responsibility for his or her own garbage, everybody wins!

When you each work your own recovery program, you are able to join each other in a new way of relating. You will find that if your husband is truly working his program, he will be more open with you than he has ever been. Men are taught that to show vulnerability is a sign of weakness. Our husbands are afraid to show us their pain for fear that their vulnerability will repel our love. But the opposite is true. When our husband trusts us enough to be vulnerable with us, he is actually more attractive. We feel loved and we want to show him more love as well.

I want you to know that if you and your husband are both willing to work your own recovery programs, it is very possible to heal your relationship. It will take time and a lot of hard work. There will be ups and downs. There will be obstacles to overcome throughout your recovery. But you can get your life back.

CHAPTER 9:
Obstacles on the Road to Recovery

Discovering my husband's porn addiction was one of the most devastating experiences of my life. At least it felt like it was at the time. When my husband made the decision to quit using porn and demonstrated his commitment to our marriage, I could finally see a glimmer of light at the end of a very dark tunnel. I had hope that I would be ok and that eventually our life would get back to normal.

A year and a half after my husband quit using porn, life seemed to be pretty good. We still had our ups and downs but we were doing all right. Our relationship wasn't perfect but it was better. I had embarked on a career change and between that and the responsibilities of motherhood, I was really busy. I was taking action toward my dreams and I was really excited for my future!

One day I was working on my computer and needed to look at my browsing history in search of a link. In that moment, the ground fell out from underneath me when I saw porn links in the current history. I went through the history with a fine-toothed comb, and I discovered my husband had been using again. He had been hiding his secret for seven months.

This relapse discovery felt even worse than the first. He knew better. He knew that our marriage almost ended because of his porn addiction, and he still chose to use porn again. I can't even begin to tell you how devastated I was. The scene played out much like it did the first time. Rising to the surface was all the self-loathing I neglected to deal with the first time. I was drowning in a swamp of emotional baggage, and he acted like a deer caught in headlights, stone-faced with no emotion, it seemed like he didn't even care.

The difference with this discovery was that I was able to regain my composure within a few days. When the dust settled from the initial storm, I was able to get my wits about me enough to start problem solving. It was clear that abstinence alone was not going to cut it. My husband's porn addiction was a much bigger problem than either of us first realized. I demanded he see our family counselor right away. When he returned from his session, I met him with an open mind.

This was a true turning point for my husband. The man who returned from that counseling session was full of remorse and allowed himself to expose his brokenness. He threw himself before me and sobbed uncontrollably for about thirty minutes. He had never before shown me even a miniscule of this kind of emotion in all the years we had been together. Without even saying a word, I could see that this addiction was as painful for him as it was for me. He was devastated by his actions and for the pain he caused me. For the first time he was able to admit that he was powerless over his porn addiction.

We did things all wrong the first time by thinking he could beat this addiction on his own. He thought he could handle it with will power, so he had no counseling and hadn't joined a recovery program. Looking back, this approach was a setup for disaster. We never really worked on any of our relationship issues. He didn't work on himself. I neglected to work on myself. We were clueless.

Relapse can be one of the biggest obstacles to your husband's recovery and to your own. But it doesn't have to be. It is equally important to understand the science behind relapse, as it is to understand the science of porn addiction. Remember that porn addiction is a dis-ease of the brain. The porn addict's brain has been rewired, and it is for this reason that relapse is a natural part of recovery. The likelihood your husband will relapse is very high. How you both perceive relapse will make all the difference in your husband's long-term recovery.

Why can't he just stop? The answer to this question has nothing to do with your husband's character, his moral fiber, his will power, or how much he loves you. Relapse happens in his brain, not in his heart. Because of what happened to his brain during the addiction process, his brain is set up for relapse.

Your husband's brain has associated certain cues with porn use. These cues could be as subtle as smells, sights, sounds or certain times of day. Maybe the smell of the perfume you would spray in the morning just before you left for the day signaling it was time to use. The act of scrolling through a seemingly harmless Facebook news feed could trigger the cues, because it simulates the action of scrolling for the perfect porn video to jerk off to.

Circumstances could be cues such as lunch breaks, business trips, or you going to bed. I can understand how cues work because I have experienced it. When I quit drinking wine, cooking dinner was a cue for me, because I often drank while cooking. Most days, six o'clock meant wine o'clock for me whether I was cooking or not. Porn addiction is not unlike any other addiction.

Because of the brain's associations to nuances that occurred in relation to porn use, these cues are likely to trigger relapse. When your husband's brain is exposed to these cues, there is an uncontrollable, automatic reflex that occurs. As a matter of fact, it happens before he is even conscious of it. This is a great reason for your husband to change his environment or his routines as best he can to avoid any cues he might be aware of. Some people have to change driving routes to avoid the strip joint they frequented, while others have changed jobs or even cities to avoid cues. The latter is, obviously, a more extreme situation. The preventative measures needed depend on the individual, but this is something you both should think about.

Remember back in chapter 2 when I talked about the *go/stop* systems? It is very important to make note of it here, as the dysfunction of these systems plays a major role in relapse. While your husband is trying to abstain from using, his *go* system still doesn't communicate with his *stop* system. When exposed to one of his cues, his brain experiences a very intense craving to use. This activates his *go* system, which bypasses his *stop* system. This means his memories of your pain and all the devastation his porn addiction has caused, are not accessible to him in that moment. When your husband is in a recovery program he will learn to rewire his brain so that the *go/stop* will function properly. But, this will take time and hard work on your husband's part.

With this in mind, you have to face the possibility of relapse. I'm going to tell you to expect it. Both you and your husband have to prepare yourselves for the inevitability of relapse so you can have a plan in place for dealing with it. Of course, you don't want it to happen. But to bury your head in the sand and ignore the possibility will not serve you or him. His recovery program will provide accountability partners who he can call when he feels the craving to use. But even that isn't a fail-safe system, so there is a still a chance your husband could relapse.

I am going to recommend you make a pact with your husband where he agrees to tell you right away if he slips (even just a click on a slightly inappropriate link), and you agree to hold a safe space for him to confess. Holding this safe space for him doesn't mean you aren't going to get mad or flip a lid. But it does mean that you will deal with it together in order to get him back on track.

My husband and I did not have any such agreement in place, and this contributed to his one slip escalating to a seven-month relapse. Fear and shame kept him from telling me right away. Because of secrecy, he could not overcome his brain's cravings and before he knew it, he was using regularly again. Your husband needs to be completely transparent and forthcoming with you as an added precaution in avoiding relapse. Don't allow secrecy to be an option.

Your emotional damage can be minimized when you use brain science to frame his relapse. If it happens, neither of you should feel defeated. There is no reason to worry that he won't beat his addiction in the long haul. Relapse is a part of his recovery, and it can provide an opportunity for your husband to better understand the triggers that set off his cravings. On a side note, relapse should not be happening on a regular basis. If it is, there is a bigger problem that needs to be addressed. The fact that relapse is normal in recovery is not an excuse for a halfhearted attempt at recovery. Tom Shelder says this about relapse:

> As with any addiction, there are triggers, which compel the addict to act out. The porn addict also has triggers and they are unique and variable to each addict. Learning these triggers and sharing them with the wife is part of the recovery process. There are often many relapses for the porn addict, especially in our culture where porn is perceived as free, easy and fulfilling. The goal is to identify triggers, communicate to the wife,

have accountability partners and set up boundaries and safety parameters so the relapses become fewer and fewer.

Now, let's talk about the shame factor. I think it is important for us to talk about shame, because it plays a major role in both your recoveries. Shame says, "I am a bad person." Guilt says, "I've done a bad thing." In order for families to heal, shame has to be taken out of porn addiction. Shame causes secrecy, and secrecy gives porn its power. Shame is why you suffer in silence, and it holds you back from asking for help. You are ashamed of your husband and of yourself for being married to him. And it is a huge reason your husband doesn't reach out for help, either. As with any addiction, there is going to be some shame. The shame related to porn addiction is way more intense than with most drugs.

Because porn addiction is a sexual dis-ease, no one wants to talk about it. No one wants to admit that porn addiction is anywhere within his or her reality. Given it is such an uncomfortable topic to talk about, it is easier to pretend it isn't there. The porn industry thrives because of this. They make billions of dollars in large part because it's embarrassing to talk about.

When I discovered my husband's porn addiction, I didn't want anyone to know. I felt ashamed that I had married a man who could stoop so low to even become a porn addict. I was ashamed because in the back of my mind, I thought there was something wrong with me. As I healed and became stronger, I talked about it with a few trusted friends. They would tell me they knew someone in the same boat who had just discovered her own husband's porn addiction, and that this person didn't know what to do. By reaching out to friends of friends and more friends of friends, my coaching practice was growing. I had never intended to build my practice by serving wives of porn addicts, it just happened. The calling chose me.

The more I speak openly about porn addiction the more women contact me. The more research I do, the more I realize there are millions of women around the world who are suffering because of their husbands' porn addiction. I work with women as far away as India, and their stories are much the same. They suffer in silence because of shame.

I am stepping out of my shame to help you step out of yours. I am here to lead you to your healing by releasing shame. I want you to know that you do not have to be ashamed. Porn is a drug. Porn addiction affects the brain just as any other drug. There is no reason to suffer in silence. I want to you understand the science of your husband's porn addiction so you can see that his addiction is a dis-ease of his brain and not of his heart. When you can remove yourself from the shame of his addiction, you will start to heal.

Knowledge is power. The more you educate yourself about porn addiction, the less power it will have over your life. Knowledge will help you heal. I know it can be scary to imagine what you might learn. When you understand the progressive nature of porn addiction it might seem really scary to know how far your husband has gone. But it does not serve you to stay in the dark. You must arm yourself with the knowledge of what porn addiction is because you need to know what you are up against. You need to know what your husband is fighting. As painful as it may be, you need to know so that you can take care of you and make the right decisions for yourself.

Don't get overwhelmed. You don't have to leap into it all at once. It is ok to take turtle steps. Take it one step at a time and only do what you can handle in the moment. You will know what you are ready for and you will know how fast or slow to go. Be careful not to let fear keep you from progressing. While you don't have to figure it all out this red-hot minute, you will eventually need to know everything. This is a process, and you need to take care of yourself along the way.

If your husband is willing to quit and is willing to commit to a recovery program, that is very good news. Some husbands may go kicking and screaming. This is a powerful addiction to overcome. His brain is going to resist recovery all the way, but that is for him to figure out. I want you to remember that your recovery does not depend on him. Regardless of what he decides, your fastest way to healing is through your own recovery program.

CHAPTER 10:

Your Happy Ending

You have been devastated by your husband's betrayal. While you may feel surrounded by darkness and unable to see your way through, there is a light at the end of the tunnel. Your path for survival has been placed in front of you. When you walk this path of recovery, you will become stronger—and you will get your life back.

I have walked this path myself, and, using this map, I have helped women like you find their way home. In the hope of shedding light on what is possible for you, I will share my story of success because everything I have accomplished is possible for you.

When you hear what I have to say next, you might think I am crazy, but I'm going to say it anyway because it is my truth. From where I sit now, I can look back at my life prior to this dreadful ordeal and I can honestly say that discovering my husband's porn addiction was one of the best things that has ever happened to me. This is what recovery has done for me.

Before discovering my husband's porn addiction, I was coasting along, living life at the level of status quo. My life was comfortable, but it could have been better. The problem with being comfortable is that I got lazy. I wasn't working on myself. When life got stressful, my old dysfunctional behaviors took over. Co-dependency started to slip in, little by little. My old painful stories were there once again, festering below the surface. I could feel them, but I didn't want to deal with them—so I started to use wine to numb my pain. I had dreams, but I didn't think I had "what it takes" to make them come true. That ship had already sailed, and it was too late for me.

My husband's porn addiction was my wake-up call! Once I was in recovery, I could see that my dysfunctional behaviors had been in charge of my life. Co-dependency and addiction were back in full swing. How the hell did that happen? I had worked through all that long ago. I thought I was "co-dependent no more" and was addiction-free when I quit my weed addiction. I had been through Al-Anon, counseling, spiritual searching, and several self-development workshops. I worked really hard on myself to break free from my first dysfunctional marriage. And here I was again, in another dysfunctional marriage. This is what happens when you fall asleep.

Crisis has a wonderful way of opening your eyes to what you do not want to see. My husband's porn addiction was my awakening. There is nothing like pain of betrayal to give you a swift kick in the butt. My pain was so intense that I knew I had to find my way out of it. It was time for me to take control of my life. I had the tools already—I just had to use them. It was time to make a commitment to myself by investing in my own healing.

This renewed commitment to recovery changed my life in the most incredible ways. I was very fortunate to work with some brilliant coaches who helped me along the way. I had done plenty of my own self-development work in the past. I knew what I needed to do. I had the tools and I knew how to use them. But there were many times when I found myself stuck and unable to move forward. I could have muddled along on my own, but I was in pain and I wanted out in a hurry. I needed a coach to throw me a lifeline and to nudge me along the way. Coaching was the accelerant my recovery needed. Because I invested in my healing, I was able to progress more quickly.

It has been just over a year since I made the decision to step on the path to recovery. It was scary to take the leap. In the beginning, I was filled with fears about my future. I knew there were things I would have to look at, and they were things I did not want to see. I would have to learn things about my husband's addiction that I was afraid to know. I was afraid to face my demons. There were so many unknowns. Some days I just wanted to pull the covers over my head and wish it all away. Other days brought moments of clarity when I knew that I had the courage to move forward. On those days, I was able to face my fears head on. And every time I did, I grew a little stronger.

Facing my fears was my way of taking back my power. My confidence grew, and I realized I was capable of much more than I gave myself credit for. Some days I felt the warrior spirit burning within me, and other days I couldn't find that inner warrior to save my life. Then I would remember what a very wise woman once told me: "Sometimes you have to fake it 'til you make it." And that is what I did.

My life came together beautifully. I did things that I thought were out of my reach. For the first time in my life, I had the courage to follow my dreams. Through recovery, I was able to start living again. My world has completely opened up. My career has taken off, and I am serving women all over the world! Every day, I look forward to my work because I love what I do. My life was not anything like this before discovering my husband's porn addiction. Working through the heartache of his betrayal has made me stronger than I have ever been. I am confident and I have a new sense of independence.

For the first time in my life, I like myself. I accept myself as I am. My happiness no longer depends on anyone or anything outside of me. My happiness comes from within me. Do I still have more work to do? Hell, yes. This process is ongoing. I know that as long as I continue working my program, I will know how to deal with whatever life throws my way.

Just recently, life provided me with the perfect opportunity to experience this new confidence in action. I was on my computer and a little voice said to look at the browser history for YouTube. I have learned to trust this voice, so I pulled up the history. More than a year after his major relapse, I saw that my husband had clicked on some questionable links. His *go* system got the better of him, but he quickly gained control. He didn't jerk off to porn.

The old me would have flown off the handle and raged on him for even looking at anything that remotely looked like porn. But the new me called him in and calmly said, "My life is taking off and I get to choose who I take with me. I will choose to leave you behind if you are an active porn addict." In that moment, I felt truly free.

My marriage is back on track and in many ways it is better than ever. I am so proud of my husband for working on his recovery. More and more, it feels like I have my husband back and he is better than he was before. He has learned to be truly intimate again.

You may not be able to see it now, but all that I have accomplished through recovery is possible for you. This is your plan for survival. Follow it, and you will be well on your way to taking your life back.

You will find helpful links on my resource page. While some of the information may seem like more than you want to know, take it in as best you can. As I said earlier, knowledge is power. Understanding that porn addiction is a dis-ease of the brain will be your first step in separating yourself from your husband's addiction. Not only will you understand how his brain is driving his addiction, but also you will better understand how and why his addiction has affected your relationship. This knowledge will help you to set clear boundaries with your husband.

Fearlessly set boundaries. This is the most important step you can take. If you take away only one thing from this book, let it be this. Throw the rest of the book away, but not before you set very clear boundaries with your husband. In chapter 2, you learned the non-negotiable boundaries that are mandatory to have in place. There are other boundaries you will want to set based on the extent of his addiction that are in line with your personal circumstances. If you need help in figuring out what those are, don't hesitate to ask for help. Clear boundaries are the best thing you can do for yourself and for your husband. Know the lines you want to draw in the sand, and be prepared to stand behind them.

Tell your husband what he needs to do to save your relationship. He may be like many husbands who will choose recovery. Or he may not. Either way, you can work on yourself and get yourself strong again so that you can make decisions from a place of strength and clarity.

Use your Inner Guidance Meter. You learned it back in chapter 3. This meter will be your best guide when making decisions. Practice it often. Use it on little decisions at first. The more you practice it, the more you will trust it. Your inner guide knows exactly what you need to do. All you have to do is to learn how to tune into it and listen to its guidance. When you are in doubt, check in with you. Drop into your body to find your answers. Your body knows your truth and it will never lie to you—unlike the negative script in your head. Your Inner Guidance Meter is a great way to determine what action will bring you closer to peace.

If you don't already have one, find a spiritual practice to use every day. It can be reading religious text, reading inspirational books, yoga, or even daily prayer. Whatever practice you choose, it doesn't have to take a big chunk out of your day. Even five minutes spent with your Higher

Power first thing in the morning can give you the strength you need to get through your day.

Spend dedicated time cleaning up your own life. Take a look at your own behavior patterns. What are you addicted to? Do you have a problem with shopping, eating, drama, or alcohol? Do you have your own stinking thinking that you need to clean up? Look at the way you treat yourself. You and I both know about the plethera of negative self-talk your husband's addiction has stirred up. Work on that. Learn to be kinder to yourself. Examine the fears that are holding you back. If you don't know where to start, go back to the exercises in chapter 5.

Work on your mindset. Learn to question your stressful thoughts. You can clear up a world of pain just by changing your thoughts. You have a choice in suffering. Refer back to chapter 6 and use the four questions and turnarounds to change your thinking. Look at your answers from the exercises in chapter 5 and question those beliefs. If you need help, ask for it.

When you are ready to let go of your pain, you will be ready to work on forgiveness. In chapter 7, I gave you a couple of options for doing this. You can pray for your husband's happiness for 30 days and/or start practicing the Ho'Oponopono prayer every day. Both of these are simple and easy with a minimum time requirement. You will be surprised at the results you get. Your husband may not change, but something in you will, and that will make a difference in how you proceed with your life.

I am stepping out of my shame and stepping up to publicly announce that I am the wife of a porn addict. It isn't easy. I have experienced resistance along the way both from within me and from outside of me as well.

People are afraid to be associated with porn addiction in any way. I belong to a personal development organization where members are encouraged to share their struggles as well as their experience, strength, and hope. In this group, people are able to talk about their addictions, being abused, their fears, and anything else they are struggling with. But when I asked to share my story, I was denied. A group that felt it safe to talk about recovery from heroin addiction and even recovery from prostitution denied me because they thought that talking about porn addiction would make other members feel unsafe. They wouldn't allow me to talk about my own recovery from thc betrayal of my husband's porn addiction. What the hell? In a group of thousands of people, I know there were plenty of women who would have been relieved to hear what I had to say.

This experience gave me pause, and I almost decided not to go public with my story. This book could have gone unwritten because of this one group's reaction. Instead, it lit a fire in me. I said, "Screw it!" I am going public because there are women who are suffering in silence, and they need my voice to show them a way out of their pain. Women are waiting to hear what I have to say. Like you, they need to know that they can survive this betrayal and that there is a clear path for recovery.

This book is for you! I am speaking up for you! You are not crazy. You did not cause your husband's porn addiction and you cannot cure it. But you can fight your way through the pain it has caused. You will feel whole again, and you will find happiness. It is time for you to get serious about recovery and take back your life

Take care of yourself! Be fearless in getting what you need. And if you need help, ask for it. You do not have to do this alone.

RESOURCES

For both of you:

What Is Addiction?, by Gabor Maté
https://youtu.be/T5sOh4gKPIg

We Need To Talk About Sex Addiction,
by Paula Hall, TEDxLeamingtonSpa
https://youtu.be/-Qf2e3XZ8Tw

Porn Addiction Resources and Accountability Software for Devices:
http://www.covenanteyes.com/
http://www.fightthenewdrug.org/

For husbands:

Terry Crews, actor and former professional football athlete talks about his porn addiction in his six-part video series, "Dirty Little Secret."
https://youtu.be/I4krRkO4sHc

Wild at Heart, by John Eldredge

Facing the Shadow, by Patrick Carnes, Ph. D.

Suggested Reading for Wives:

Loving What Is, by Byron Katie
www.thework.com

A Return to Love, by Marianne Williamson

The Four Agreements, by Don Miguel Ruiz

Your Sexually Addicted Spouse, by Barbara Steffens

Facing Heartbreak, by Stephanine Carnes, Mari A. Lee, and Anthony Rodriquez

Mending a Shattered Heart, by Stephanine Carnes

Partners: Healing from His Addiction, by Dr. Doug Weiss

Moving Beyond Betrayal, by Vicki Tidwell Palmer

ACKNOWLEDGEMENTS

Where would a girl be without her mom? I don't think I would have had the courage to write this book if it weren't for my mom, Lois Brown, who taught me that I could do anything I set my mind to. She always believed in me when I didn't believe in myself. My mom taught me many valuable lessons growing up, the most important being: "No matter how hard life gets, don't let it keep you down; pick yourself up, face your fears, and move forward courageously."

I have carried this lesson my entire life, and it helped me survive the pain of my husband's betrayal. Without my mom, I might not be here now, showing other women how to survive betrayal and take their life back. Thanks, Mom. I love you a bushel and a peck.

It goes without saying I wouldn't have written *Porn Addict's Wife* if it weren't for my husband Ted, and his porn addiction. What initially felt like the worst thing that had ever happened "to" me, turned out to be the best thing "for" me. Having to fight my way through the pain of betrayal helped me to grow and heal in ways I would never have imagined. For the first time in my life I am doing what I need to do to make my dreams come true. Recovery has made us both stronger people and our marriage gets better and better because of it.

Thank you, Ted, for committing to do whatever it takes to repair our relationship. If you hadn't, our story would be much different. I respect your dedication to recovery, and I can see the results of your hard work. It is a blessing to see you become a stronger, healthier and happier man. You are an example for our sons to see that when a man takes responsibility for his mistakes, he becomes a better man. You, Ted, are becoming a better man and because of it, I love you more each day.

Big thanks to Jana Rockne, who steered me in the direction of becoming a Life Coach. This was something I had dreamed of some time ago but I thought it was too late for me. Jana helped me realize it is never too late to follow your dreams.

I have to thank my coach, Lea Ann Mallet, for helping me discover my superpower. We often overlook our qualities and strengths that make us unique. Lea Ann helped me realize that my experience as a porn addict's wife was more than just a rough patch in my life; it was a gift that needed to be shared with women who were suffering as I did, and that by sharing my path to recovery, I could make a difference in their lives.

The Universe truly works in miraculous ways. I sincerely believe that God puts in our path the people we need at just the right time. Maureen Doyle, my new friend, fellow coach, and author of *When Your Ex Doesn't Follow The Rules,* is one of those people for me. Because she made the bold decision to write a book, I was inspired to entertain the idea that I too might do the same, sometime in the distant future. She introduced me to Angela Lauria, and as they say, "that was all she wrote." Thank you, Maureen, for showing me the way and for walking with me on this incredible journey to becoming an author. Your support and encouragement along the way have meant the world to me. Oddly enough, during this process, there was a few times when I needed your sage advice to deal with my ex who doesn't follow the rules. God blessed me when he brought you into my life. Forever friends we shall be.

This brings me to my publisher, Angela Lauria. Thank you, thank you, thank you from the bottom of my heart. You spent so much time with me on our initial calls when I thought I was "just researching" the possibilities of writing a book. You convinced me not to wait because there were women who needed my book, now. Thank you for encouraging me to believe that with my book, I could make a difference in the world. This experience has transformed my life. You are brilliant at what you do and I thank you for providing your outstanding team that makes up Difference Press. You all ROCK!

Oh what a difference an editor makes. Thank you, Maggie McReynolds. You are a consummate pro! Through your wisdom and guidance, I became the author I had always dreamed I would be. Thank you for getting me here. I couldn't have done it without you.

I would be remiss if I didn't thank the extraordinary sexual addiction specialist, Tom Shelder. I cannot praise you enough for your dedication and service to your clients. You have helped my husband transform his life, and because of your work together, Ted and I have been able to save our marriage. I can't express how much it means to have my husband back! You have made a difference in our lives as you do in the lives of so many others. And you keep on giving. Thank you for your contribution to my book, I know your wisdom will make a difference in the lives of my readers.

To my amazing sons, your encouragement has meant the world to me. Most boys your age would be embarrassed that their mom was writing a book about porn addiction, but not you guys! I can't tell you how much it means to hear you say, "I'm proud of you, Mom." It makes me cry just thinking about your words. You guys make me so proud to be your mom. You are my sunshine and I love you to the sun and back.

Thank you, Morgan James Publishing. It has been a pleasure working with your team in getting my book to print and into the hands of those who desperately need it. Special thanks to David Hancock, CEO &

Founder for believing in me and my message. To Megan Malone, thanks for all your guidance and help in making this process seamless and easy. Many more thanks to everyone else, but especially Jim Howard, Bethany Marshall, and Nickcole Watkins.

ABOUT THE AUTHOR

Sandy Brown brings over 20 years of personal development experience to her work with clients worldwide to create happier lives. She sees her own life as a work in progress and, through her own relationships, has learned to embrace both the good and the bad as opportunities for personal growth.

At the heart of Sandy's work is her belief that healthy relationships are the key to a happy life, and that our most important relationship is the one we have with ourselves. When our relationship with Self is strong and clear, it positively impacts our relationships with everything else, including money, food, exercise, work, and others. Sandy believes that happiness is an inside out job.

#1 International Best Selling Author, Certified Life and Relationship Coach specializing in Betrayal Recovery, Sandy shares that it is her own experience in surviving the betrayal of her husband's porn addiction that inspired her to focus her practice on helping other women to do the same. Through her own recovery and her experience with clients, Sandy has developed a process of recovery to empower women at a time when they feel all is lost.

Sandy and her husband are happily married and live on the shores of Lake Michigan, where they have raised their five sons.

THANK YOU

Thanks for reading *Porn Addict's Wife.* Reaching the end of this book is just the beginning of your journey through recovery. The fact that you have gotten to this point in the book tells me that you are ready to take your first steps in taking back your life.

To support you in getting started, I have created a companion video series that goes with this book.

Free Video Series: To access the companion videos for *Porn Addict's Wife*, go to www.sandybrowncoaching.com/paw-bonus

Remember, this is a journey to be taken one step at a time. You will survive this betrayal and you will take back your life! If you need help along the way you can reach me at www.talktosandybrown.com to schedule a free call.

www.TheMorganJamesSpeakersGroup.com

We connect Morgan James published authors with live and online events and audiences whom will benefit from their expertise.

Morgan James makes all of our titles available through the Library for All Charity Organization.

www.LibraryForAll.org

Printed in the USA
CPSIA information can be obtained
at www.ICGtesting.com
JSHW082351140824
68134JS00020B/2009

9 781683 503835